Easy Word
for Windows™

Shelley O'Hara

Library of Congress Catalog Number: 92-60270

ISBN: 0-88022-922-5

94   93   92   6   5   4   3   2   1

Interpretation of the printing code: the rightmost double-digit number is the year of the book's printing; the rightmost single-digit number, the number of the book's printing. For example, a printing code of 92-1 shows that the first printing of the book occurred in 1992.

Screen reproductions in this book were created using Collage Plus from Inner Media, Inc., Hollis, NH.

Easy Word for Windows is based on Microsoft Word for Windows Version 2.0.

Publisher: Lloyd J. Short

Acquisitions Manager: Rick Ranucci

Project Development Manager: Thomas H. Bennett

Book Design: Scott Cook

Production Team: Claudia Bell, Scott Boucher, Brad Chinn, Linda Quigley, Caroline Roop, Sandra Shay, Angie Trzepacz, Sue Vandewalle, Mary Beth Wakefield, Phil Worthington

Production Editor

    Laura Wirthlin

Technical Editor

    Paul Rodgers

Novice Reviewer

    Stacey Beheler

Contents at a Glance

Contents

Easy **Word for Windows**

Contents

Introduction

What Is Word for Windows?

Word for Windows is one of the most powerful word processing programs for Windows. You can use the program to create a variety of documents:

- Letters
- Memos
- Reports
- Manuscripts
- Term papers
- Legal documents

- Proposals
- Outlines
- Press releases
- Resumes
- Form letters

The next few pages provide examples of some of these documents.

Memo

To: Sales

From: Michael R. O'Hara

Date: 7/16/92

Subject: June Sales Figures

_____

Here are the sales figures by region:

Northwest	$12,000
Southwest	$24,000
Midwest	$38,000
East	$52,000
South	$23,000

You can create the same kinds of documents by using a typewriter, but Word for Windows makes writing, editing, and printing easier. Specifically, you can use Word for Windows to

6/18/92

Raymond N. Ball
5301 North Main Street
Indianapolis IN 46208

Mrs. Eugenia Frances
School 83
5050 East 82nd Street
Indianapolis IN

Dear Mrs. Frances:

I have been a teacher in the IPS school system for over 30 years. During my tenure, I had an exemplary record—for attendance, for willingness to help out, and for excellence in coaching. The numerous championship teams (softball, track, and basketball) that I coached at both School 83 and School 43 afforded these schools and the students a sense of pride unmatched. The colleagues and previous supervisors with whom I have worked can vouch for my dedication and concern for the students.

I have enjoyed my responsibilities as a teacher. But due to health reasons, I am retiring as of this year.

Sincerely,

Raymond N. Ball

Correct errors. When you press a typewriter key, you commit that letter to paper. To correct a mistake, you have to use correction fluid or retype the document. With Word for Windows, you see everything you type on-screen. You can easily correct any typographical errors before you print the document.

Move around quickly. With a document on-screen, you can move from one sentence, paragraph, or page to another. You can quickly move from the beginning of the document to the end and vice versa.

Make editing changes. You can insert text in any location in a document. You also can delete text quickly—a character, a word, a sentence, a paragraph, or any other amount of text.

Rearrange the text. When you sit down to write, you don't always write in order—from the introduction to the summary. As you are writing the summary, for example, you may think of an idea that belongs in the introduction. With Word for Windows, you can easily move or copy text from one location to another.

Curriculum Vitae
Darlene J. Gerdt

Home:	8555 Sugar Street	Office:	1800 North Main Street
	Indianapolis, IN		Suite B
	(317) 555-5331		Indianapolis, IN 46202
			(317) 555-5411

Personal

Born:	September 12, 1944
Married:	January 1964
Husband:	Ray
Children:	Kimberly L. (May 13, 1968)
	Richelle E. (June 17, 1972)

Education

College:	Indiana University
	1961-1964 (A.B.)
Medical School:	Indiana University, School of Medicine
	1964-1968 (M.D.)
Internship:	Straight Surgery
	Indiana University School of Medicine
	1968-1969
Residency:	Neurosurgery
	Indiana University Hospitals
	1971-1976

Career

Private Practice:	IMG
	1976 to present
Clinical Appointments:	St. Jude Hospital of Indiana, Inc.
	St. George Hospital and Health Care Center
	Women's Hospital
	City Hospital North
Teaching Appointments:	Clinical Assistant Professor of Surgery (Neurosurgery)
	Indiana University Medical Center
Research:	Investigator
	International Cooperative Study of Aneurysms and Subarachnoid Hemorrhage
	1987 to present
Specialty Certification:	American Board of Neurological Surgery
	May 1980

Victorian Home Tour

July 16 - 18
9AM to 5PM
Irvington

Call 555-1980 for ticket information.

The Marriage Trifecta

Chapter 6
No Keepsies

My family always had their fingers in my love pie. Fixing this one up, ruining that one. When I was seven, we went to Virginia Beach, and they tried to pawn me off on some fat kid. My mom spotted him and thought it would be nice if I played with him. This nice boy had a burr hair cut and looked like a Weeble. Weebles wobble, but they don't fall down. Mom dubbed him Sluggo and invited him to our hotel room to play. When he knocked on the door, I hid under the bed, but my sister grabbed my ankles and pulled me out.

Sluggo had just been to Williamsburg and had a bag full of marbles. He said he'd teach me how to play, but he stressed we were playing for "no keepsies." This meant that if I won and knocked the marbles out of the circle, I couldn't keep them. As I slaughtered him at marbles, all Sluggo could say was "Remember, no keepsies. No keepsies." When I reported back to my mom about the marble date, she got the biggest kick out of that phrase "no keepsies" that she repeated "Sluggo" and "no keepsies" throughout the rest of the vacation--actually, the rest of my life.

Restore deleted text. If you accidentally delete text you want to keep, you don't have to retype it. Instead, you can simply restore the text.

Check spelling. Before you print a document, you can run a "spell check" to search for misspellings and double words. If you are a poor typist, you can leave spelling errors for Word for Windows to catch. You can concentrate on writing rather than on spelling.

Search for text. You can search a document for a particular word or phrase. For example, you can move quickly to the section of a document that discusses expenditures by searching for the word *expenditures*.

Search for and replace text. You can make replacements throughout a document quickly and easily. For example, you can change all occurrences of the word *Spokesman* to *Presenter*.

Make formatting changes. You can easily change margins, tabs, and other formatting options. You can experiment with the settings until the document appears the way you want it. Then, you can print the final version.

Change how text appears. You can make text bold, italic, and so on. You also can use different fonts, depending on your printer.

Preview a document. You can preview a document to see how it will look when printed. If necessary, you can make changes before you print the document.

Copy and reuse a document. You can make a duplicate copy of a document and then make changes to create a second, different document.

Why You Need This Book

Word for Windows' features make working with text easy. Using this program saves you time and makes your work more efficient. But learning to use the program's many features can be difficult at first—that's why you need this book.

This book is designed to make learning Word for Windows easy. *Easy Word for Windows* helps the beginning Word for Windows user perform basic operations. Following the step-by-step instructions, you can learn how to take advantage of Word for Windows' editing and formatting options.

You don't have to worry that you don't know enough about computers or about Word for Windows to use the program. This book teaches you all you need to know.

You don't have to worry that you might do something wrong and ruin a document or the computer. This book points out mistakes you might make and shows you how to avoid them. This book also explains what to do when you change your mind and tells you how to escape from a situation.

Reading *Easy Word for Windows* will build your confidence with Word for Windows. You will learn how to perform the tasks you need to get a particular job done.

How This Book Is Organized

Easy Word for Windows is designed with you, the beginner, in mind. The book is divided into several parts:

- Introduction
- The Basics
- Task/Review
- Reference

This part, the Introduction, explains how the book is organized and how to use the book.

The next part, The Basics, outlines general information about the computer and its keyboard. The Basics part also explains basic Word for Windows concepts such as moving around a document, selecting commands, and understanding the screen display.

The main portion of this book, the Task/Review part, tells you how to perform particular tasks. The first task explains how to start the program.

Each task includes numbered steps that tell you how to complete a specific sample exercise. The exercise is illustrated with Before and After screens. The review provides the general steps you follow to complete the task. You can apply the numbered steps in the review to your own tasks.

The last part, Reference, includes a quick reference guide to the most commonly used features, a keyboard guide, and a glossary. The glossary provides definitions of computer terms and terms that apply to Word for Windows.

How To Use This Book

This book is set up so that you can use it in several different ways:

- You can read the book from start to finish.
- You can start reading at any point in the book.
- You can experiment with one task, many tasks, or all tasks.
- You can look up specific tasks you want to accomplish, such as making text bold.
- You can flip through the book, looking at the Before and After screens, to find specific tasks.
- You can look through the alphabetical listing of tasks at the beginning of the Task/Review part to find a task.
- You can read just the task, just the review, or both the task and review. As you learn the program, you may want to follow along with the tasks. After you learn the program, you can use the review to remind yourself how to perform a certain task.
- You can read any part of the exercises you want. You can read all of the text to see the steps you follow and the explanations of those steps. You can read only the

text in red to see the commands you select and the keys you press. You can read just the explanation to understand what happens during a particular step.

How To Follow an Exercise

Word for Windows is flexible because it enables you to perform a task in many different ways. For consistency, this book makes certain assumptions about how your computer is set up and how you use Word for Windows. As you follow each exercise, keep the following key points in mind:

- This book assumes that you followed the basic installation instructions. This book also assumes that you have installed a printer and that you have not changed any program defaults. (For further explanations of your computer system, see *Understanding Your Computer System* in the Basics part. For help on installing the program, see *Using Word for Windows 2,* Special Edition.)

- This book assumes that you use the mouse to move the insertion point, select text, select menu commands, and so on. Remember that you also can accomplish these tasks by using the keyboard. (See the *Keyboard Guide* in the Reference part.)

- In the Task/Review part, this book assumes that you are starting from the Before screen. If the Before screen contains any text, you should type the text that appears in this screen.

- Only the Before and After screens are illustrated. This book does not show you screens for every step within an exercise. Where necessary, the explanations discuss screen messages and how to respond to them. So that the text in the screens is readable, this book uses a large font size. Depending on the font you use, your screen and line breaks might appear differently.

Task section

The Task section includes numbered steps that tell you how to accomplish certain tasks, such as copying text or printing a document. The numbered steps walk you through a specific example so that you can learn the task by doing it. Blue text below each numbered step explains the concept in more detail.

Oops! notes

You may find that you performed a task that you do not want after all. The Oops! notes tell you how to undo a procedure or get out of a situation. By showing you how to reverse nearly every procedure, these notes enable you to use Word for Windows more confidently.

TASK

before

Copy text

Seminar Schedule

Monday

8:30   Speaker: Learning Word for Windows Basics
10:30   Questions and Answers
11:30   Lunch

Tuesday

8:30   Speaker: Putting Word for Windows To Work

Wednesday

Oops!
To delete the copied text, select the Edit Undo Paste command immediately after pasting the text. Or, just delete the copied text.

1. Click before the *10* in *10:30*.
   This step places the insertion point at the beginning of the text you want to copy.

2. Select the next two lines (the line that begins with *10:30* and the line that begins with *11:30*).
   You can use the mouse or the keyboard to select the text. To use the mouse, click at the beginning of the text, hold down the left mouse button, drag across the text you want to select, and then release the mouse button. To use the keyboard, place the insertion point at the beginning of the text, hold down the Shift key, use the arrow keys to select the text, and then release the Shift key. See *TASK: Select text* for more information.

3. Point to **Edit** in the menu bar and click the left mouse button.
   This step opens the Edit menu. You see a list of Edit commands.

4. Point to **Copy** and click the left mouse button.
   This step selects the Copy command. Word for Windows copies the text to the Clipboard. (The Clipboard is a temporary holding area for text and graphics.)

5. Click on the blank line between *8:30* and *Wednesday*.
   This step places the insertion point where you want the copied text to appear.

68

Easy Word for Windows

Easy **Word for Windows**

Before and After screens

Each task includes Before and After screens that show how the computer screen looks before and after you follow the numbered steps in the Task section.

Review section

After you learn a procedure by following a specific example, you can refer to the Review section for a quick summary of the task. The Review section gives you the more generic steps for completing a task so that you can apply the steps to your own work. You can use these steps as a quick reference to refresh your memory about how to perform a procedure.

after

6. Point to **Edit** in the menu bar and click the left mouse button.
   This step opens the Edit menu again.

7. Point to **Paste** and click the left mouse button.
   This step selects the Paste command. The copied text now appears in the new location (as well as the original location).

Select, then do
Word for Windows follows the principle of select, then do. Before you can copy, move, or format text, you must select that text.

REVIEW

1. Select the text you want to copy.
2. Click on **Edit** in the menu bar.
3. Click on the **Copy** command.
4. Place the insertion point where you want the copy of the text to appear.
5. Click on **Edit** in the menu bar.
6. Click on the **Paste** command.

To copy text

Keyboard shortcuts
Press the Ctrl+C or Ctrl+Ins key combination to select the Edit Copy command. Press the Ctrl+V or Shift+Ins key combination to select the Edit Paste command.

Other notes

The extra margin notes explain a little more about the procedure. These notes define terms, explain other options, and refer you to other sections, when applicable.

Entering and Editing Text

69

Where To Get More Help

This book does not cover all Word for Windows features or all ways to complete a task. This book is geared toward the beginning Word for Windows user—a user who wants just the basics. This user isn't ready for advanced features such as using styles or creating columns. This book covers just the most common, basic features.

As you become more comfortable using Word for Windows, you may want a more complete reference book. Que offers several books to suit your needs:

> *Using Word for Windows 2,* Special Edition
>
> *Word for Windows 2 QuickStart*

Also of interest:

> *Using Microsoft Windows 3.1,* Special Edition
>
> *Easy Windows,* 3.1 Edition
>
> *Que's Computer User's Dictionary,* 2nd Edition
>
> *Introduction to Personal Computers,* 2nd Edition

The Basics

Understanding Your Computer System

Using a Mouse

Using Your Keyboard

Understanding the Document Window

Selecting a Menu Command

Moving the Insertion Point

Typing Text

Saving and Retrieving Your Work

Understanding Key Terms

Easy Word for Windows

This part explains basic information you need to know to use Word for Windows. In particular, this part

- Explains the parts of a computer system
- Discusses how to use a mouse
- Discusses the keyboard
- Describes the document window
- Explains how to select a menu command
- Explains how to type and select text
- Discusses the importance of saving your work
- Defines key terms

Understanding Your Computer System

Think of your computer as just another appliance. Even though each model is different, all computers have similar parts. You probably can figure out how to use any toaster. After you start using a computer, you should be able to figure out how to use any computer.

Your computer system is made up of these basic parts:

- The system unit
- The monitor
- The keyboard
- The floppy disk drive(s)
- The hard disk drive

You probably also have a mouse and a printer.

System Unit. This is the box that holds all the electrical components of your computer. (The size of the system unit varies.) Somewhere on this box, you can find a power switch. The location and name of this switch— I/O, Power, and so on—also varies. If you have trouble finding the switch, check your computer manual.

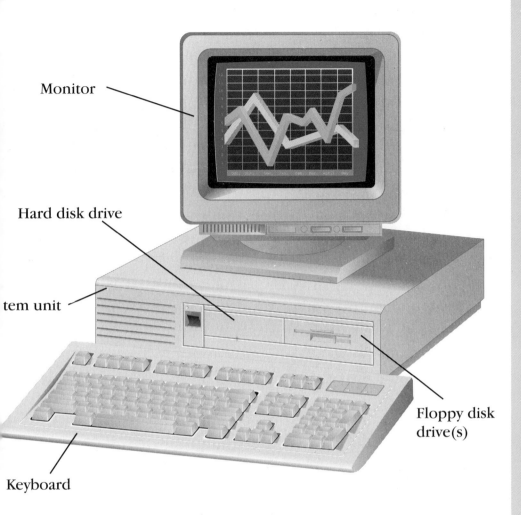

Monitor

Hard disk drive

tem unit

Floppy disk
drive(s)

Keyboard

Monitor. The monitor displays on-screen whatever you type
on the keyboard. Your monitor may have a separate
power switch.

Keyboard. You use the keyboard to communicate with the
computer. You use it to type entries and to issue
commands. You type on the keyboard just as you type
on a regular typewriter. A keyboard also has special
keys. (Different computers have different special keys.)
These keys are discussed in the section *Using Your
Keyboard*.

Floppy Disk Drive. The floppy disk drive is the door into your computer. The floppy disk drive enables you to put information onto the computer—onto the hard drive—and to take information off the computer—onto a floppy disk.

Hard Disk Drive. A hard disk drive drive stores the programs and files with which you work. To use Word for Windows, you must have a hard disk drive.

Printer. To print your documents, you need to attach and install a printer. Installing a printer tells Word for Windows what model of printer you have.

Mouse. You use the mouse, a pointing device, to move the insertion point, select text, select menu commands, and so on.

Using a Mouse

Using a mouse is the easiest and most natural way to learn Word for Windows and other Windows programs. This book assumes that you are using a mouse. (Basic techniques for using the keyboard are covered in the *Keyboard Guide*.)

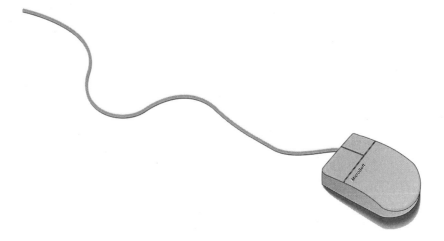

When you slide the mouse on your desk, the *mouse pointer* moves on-screen. You can use the mouse to

- Select menu commands (see *Selecting a Menu Command*)

- Select text (see *Selecting Text*)

There are four types of mouse actions:

Point. Place the mouse pointer on an item.

Click. Point to an item and then press and release the left mouse button one time.

Double-click. Point to an item and then press and release the left mouse button two times in rapid succession.

Drag. Point to an item. Press and hold down the left mouse button and then slide the mouse. When the item you are dragging is where you want it to be, release the mouse button.

Keep these terms in mind as you follow a task.

If you double-click on an item and nothing happens, you may have clicked too slowly. Try again.

Using Your Keyboard

A computer keyboard is just like a typewriter, except that a keyboard has additional keys:

- Function keys such as F1

- Arrow keys

- Other special keys such as Esc, Del, and Ins

These keys are located in different places on different keyboards. For example, sometimes the function keys are across the top of the keyboard and sometimes they are on the left side of the keyboard.

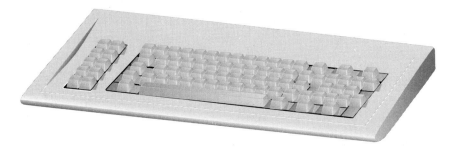

Original PC Keyboard

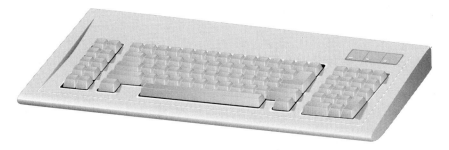

AT Keyboard

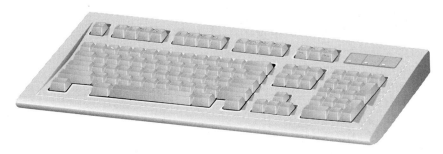

Enhanced Keyboard

Your keyboard has most, if not all, of the same keys as these keyboards, but the keys may be in different locations. You can become familiar with your keyboard by reading the names that appear on its keys.

The Function Keys

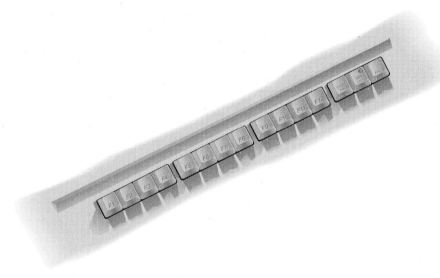

If you want, you can use the function keys (rather than the mouse) to select some commands. Pressing F12, for example, selects the File Save As command. For some commands, you use a *key combination*—a function key and a modifier key.

Shift is an example of a modifier key. You probably are familiar with the Shift key from using a typewriter. For example, you press Shift and t to create a different letter—an uppercase T. You can use the Shift key in the same way with function keys— you press Shift and a function key to access a different command than the function key alone.

Alt and Ctrl are also modifier keys. They work just like Shift. Pressing Alt and a function key, for example, accesses a different command than pressing the function key alone.

To press a key, just tap the key one time. (Some keys repeat if you hold them down too long.) To use a key combination, press and hold down the first key and then press (and release) the second key. This book indicates a key combination with a plus sign.

Keyboard shortcuts for selecting menu commands appear on the Word for Windows menus. In addition, this book lists some shortcuts in the exercises and in the *Quick Reference Guide*.

The Arrow Keys

You also can use the keyboard to move the insertion point (see *Moving the Insertion Point*).

Your keyboard may have two sets of arrow keys and editing keys (the Del and Ins keys). You may have one set to the right of the alphanumeric keys and another set on the numeric keypad. You can use either set of keys.

Other Special Keys

Here's a short list of other special keys on a computer keyboard:

Key	Function
Backspace	Deletes the character to the left of the insertion point.
Delete	Deletes the character to the right of the insertion point.
Esc	Enables you to back out of a situation—to close a menu without making a selection, to close a dialog box, and so on.
Shift	In combination with the arrow keys, enables you to select text.

Understanding the Document Window

When you start the program, Word for Windows displays a blank document window. If you want to start the program and follow along, see *TASK: Start Word for Windows*. This task is the first exercise in the Task/Review part.

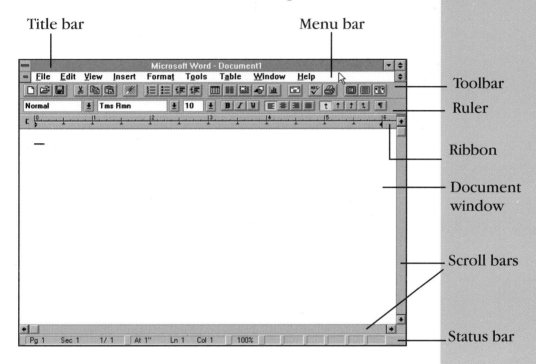

Here are some important areas of the screen:

- Title bar
- Menu bar
- Toolbar
- Ruler
- Ribbon
- Document window
- Status bar
- Scroll bars

The title bar at the top of the screen displays the name of the document. If you haven't saved (and named) the document, Document1 appears in the title bar.

The menu bar is just below the title bar. This line displays the main menu names (File, Edit, View, Insert, Format, Tools, Table, Window, and Help). To select a menu command, see *Selecting a Menu Command*.

The next three option bars (the Toolbar, the ribbon, and the ruler) enable you to select commands and make formatting changes quickly. The Toolbar, the ribbon, and the ruler appear when you start Word for Windows.

The Toolbar provides buttons for selecting frequently used commands. To start the Speller, for example, you can simply click on the button with ABC and a check mark. You can turn on and off the display of the Toolbar (see *TASK: Hide Toolbar*).

The ribbon enables you to make formatting changes quickly—to change alignment, to make text bold, and so on. The ruler enables you to make other formatting changes—for example, to change tabs and margins. You can turn on and off the display of the ribbon and ruler (see *TASK: Hide the ribbon* and *TASK: Hide the ruler*).

Note: Depending on the changes you have made, you may or may not see the Toolbar, ribbon, and ruler on-screen.

The document window appears under the Toolbar, the ribbon, and the ruler. This is the area where you type text.

The status bar appears at the bottom of the screen. This line displays messages, the location of the insertion point, the page number, and other information.

The scroll bars appear at the right side and bottom of the screen. You can use these bars to scroll through the document. To scroll one line at a time, click the *scroll arrow* at the top or bottom of the vertical scroll bar. To scroll continuously, click the scroll arrow and hold down the mouse button. To scroll more quickly, drag the *scroll box* (the box that appears on the scroll bar somewhere between the scroll arrows) up or down the scroll bar.

Selecting a Menu Command

You access commands through Word for Windows' menu system. Click on the name of the menu you want to open— for example, File. Word for Windows displays a list of commands. Click on the command you want to use.

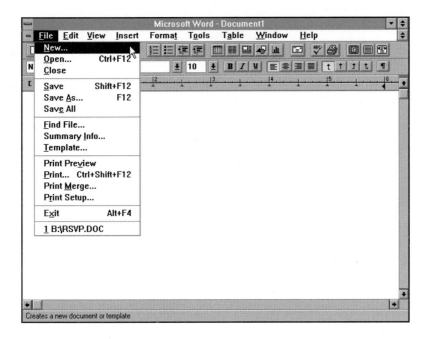

You also can use the keyboard to select menu commands. See the *Keyboard Guide*.

Sometimes you may open a menu that doesn't have the command you want to use. To leave a menu without making a selection, press the Esc key.

If a command is followed by an ellipsis (...), you must specify additional options before you initiate the command. When you select the command, Word for Windows displays a dialog box. The dialog box may ask you to enter text, make a choice about options, or confirm an operation. For example, when you select the File Open command, you see the Open dialog box.

text box   list box   command buttons

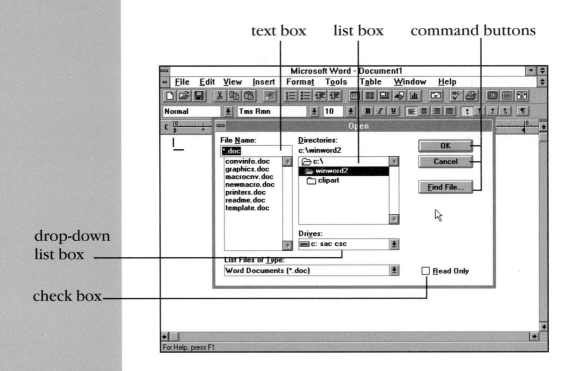

drop-down
list box

check box

Dialog boxes can contain different elements. Each item may
require a different type of selection process. Here are some
of the most common elements:

text box. A box where you type information—such as a
file name. To select a text box, click inside the box.
(Sometimes the insertion point is already in the text
box.)

check box. A square box that appears to the left of an
option. To select or deselect the option, you check
(select) or uncheck (deselect) its check box. To select a
check box, click on the box. To deselect a check box,
click on the box again.

list box. A box that contains a list of available choices—such
as file names or directories. To select an item in a list
box, click on the item. Sometimes list boxes have scroll
bars you can use to scroll through the list.

drop-down list box. Some list boxes display just the first
item. To display other items in the list, click on the
down arrow next to the drop-down list box.

Easy **Word for Windows**

option button. A round button that appears to the left of an option. To select the option, click on its option button. When an option is active, a dot appears in the button. You cannot activate more than one option in a group of option buttons. Some dialog boxes have more than one group of option buttons, but other dialog boxes (such as the Open dialog box) do not have any option buttons.

command button. A button that performs an action. Two common command buttons are OK and Cancel. To select a command button, click on the button. Most dialog boxes have a "default" command or option button. To select this button, you also can press Enter.

Moving the Insertion Point

To move the insertion point by using the mouse, click the location where you want to place the insertion point.

Note that if nothing appears in the document window, you cannot move the insertion point. Word for Windows does not permit you to move the insertion point where nothing exists. After you type text in the document window, you can move the insertion point.

You also can use the arrow keys and other key combinations to move the insertion point. Here is a list of the most common keys:

To move	Press
One character right	→
One character left	←
One line up	↑
One line down	↓
To the end of the preceding word	Ctrl+←
To the beginning of the next word	Ctrl+→
To the beginning of the line	Home

continues

To move	Press
To the end of line	End
To the beginning of the document	Ctrl+Home
To the end of the document	Ctrl+End

Typing Text

To enter text, just start typing. The alphanumeric keys work just as they do on a typewriter. Instead of committing the characters to paper, though, you see what you type on-screen.

Note that unlike a typewriter, you do not have to press Enter when you reach the end of a line. If Word for Windows can't fit a word on a line, it moves that word to the beginning of the next line. This feature is called *word wrap*.

Correcting Typos

Because you can see on-screen what you type on the keyboard, you can easily spot and correct any mistakes.

To insert text, move the insertion point to that location and type the text you want to add. Word for Windows inserts new text and moves existing text to the right. Do not press the Ins key to insert text.

To delete text, move the insertion point to the left of the character you want to delete and press the Del key. Or, move the insertion point to the right of the text you want to delete and press the Backspace key. You can use other methods to delete sentences, words, or even whole pages. See the Task/Review part for step-by-step information.

Inserting Blank Lines

You don't have to press Enter at the end of a line, but you do press Enter to end a paragraph. To insert a blank line between paragraphs, just press Enter again.

Selecting Text

When you want to work with several lines of text, you first select the text. You can select text by using the mouse or the keyboard.

To select text by using the mouse, place the mouse pointer where you want to begin selecting, hold down the left mouse button, drag across the text you want to select, and then release the mouse button.

To select text by using the keyboard, place the insertion point where you want to begin selecting, hold down the Shift key, and then press the arrow keys to select the text. See *TASK: Select text* for more information.

Word for Windows highlights the text you select.

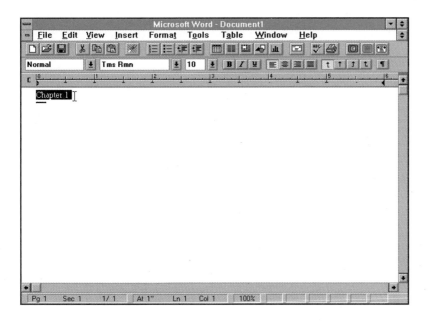

Saving and Retrieving Your Work

The computer temporarily stores all your work in memory. This process is similar to creating a shopping list in your head—until you commit the shopping list to paper, you may forget some or all of the items. The same is true with Word for Windows—until you save the document, you can lose part or all of your work.

Saving the document doesn't commit it to paper like writing down a shopping list. Saving the document stores the document on disk. Then, when you need the document again, you can retrieve it from the disk.

Word for Windows does not automatically save your work, so you should save it every five or ten minutes. If you don't save your work, you could lose it. Suppose that you have been working on a document for a few hours. Then your power goes off unexpectedly—an air conditioning repair man at your office shorts out the power, a thunderstorm hits, or whatever (any number of things can cause a power loss). If you haven't saved, you will lose all your hard work.

Note: You can turn on an automatic save feature that saves your work periodically. See *Using Word for Windows 2*, Special Edition, for information.

You have many choices when you save a document. Refer to these tasks:

When you want to	Refer to
Save a document you have not saved	*Task: Save a document for the first time*
Open a document you have saved	*Task: Open an existing document*
Save a document you saved before	*Task: Save a document again*
Save a document with a new name and keep the original	*Task: Save a document with a new name*
Start a new document	*Task: Create a new document*
Clear the screen and abandon the document on-screen; return to the previous version (if you have saved) or lose the current version (if you haven't saved)	*Task: Abandon a document*
Clear the screen, but save the document	*Task: Save and close a document*

Understanding Key Terms

Here is a list of key terms you should understand:

dialog box. A window that displays additional command options. Many times a dialog box reminds you of the consequence or result of a command and asks you to confirm that you want to go ahead with the action.

directory. An index to the files stored on disk or a list of files. A directory is similar to a file cabinet; you can group files together in directories.

document window. The area in which you type text. You can have more than one document window open at one time.

file. The various individual reports, memos, databases, letters, and so on that you store on your hard disk (or floppy disks) for future use. The actual Word for Windows program is also stored in a file.

hard return. A code the program inserts in the document when you press Enter. You use hard returns to end paragraphs or to insert blank lines.

insertion point. A flashing vertical line that indicates where you will begin typing text, deleting text, selecting text, and so on.

ribbon. An on-screen option bar that enables you to make formatting changes (to change the font, font size, font style, and alignment). You can turn on or off the display of the ribbon.

ruler. An on-screen option bar that enables you to make formatting changes (to change tabs, indents, and margins). You can turn on or off the display of the ruler.

Toolbar. An on-screen option bar that contains buttons that access commonly used commands. You can turn on or off the display of the Toolbar.

word wrap. A feature that eliminates the need to press Enter each time you reach the right margin. Instead, Word for Windows "wraps" the word to the next line automatically.

Task/Review

Entering and Editing Text

Managing Files

Formatting

Advanced Editing and Formatting

Printing

Easy Word for Windows

Alphabetical Listing of Tasks

Easy **Word for Windows**

Entering and Editing Text

This section covers the following tasks:

Start Word for Windows

Select a menu command

Exit Word for Windows

Get help

Hide the Toolbar

Hide the ruler

Display the ribbon

Add text

Overwrite text

Insert a blank line

Combine paragraphs

Insert a tab

Enter a page break

Go to a page

Select text

Delete text

Copy text

Move text

Use Undo

Start Word for Windows

before

```
C:\>
```

Oops!
Be sure to double-click on the icon. If nothing happens (or if the icon slides around), try double-clicking again.

1. **Turn on the computer and monitor.**
   Every computer has a different location for its power switch. Check the sides, the front, and the back of your system unit. Your monitor may have a separate power switch; if so, turn on your monitor.

2. **If necessary, respond to the prompts for date and time.**
   Some systems ask you to enter the current date and time when you turn on the computer. Many newer models enter the time and date automatically. If your computer doesn't prompt you for these entries, don't worry.

   If your computer does prompt you, type the current date and press Enter. Then, type the current time and press Enter.

3. **Type win and press Enter.**
   Win is the command to start Microsoft Windows. You see the Program Manager on-screen. The Program Manager is an application that comes with Microsoft Windows.

4. **Double-click on the group icon for Word for Windows.**
   To double-click, click the left mouse button two times in rapid succession. This step opens the Word for Windows program group. (In Microsoft Windows, programs are stored in groups.) If the program group is already open, you can skip this step.

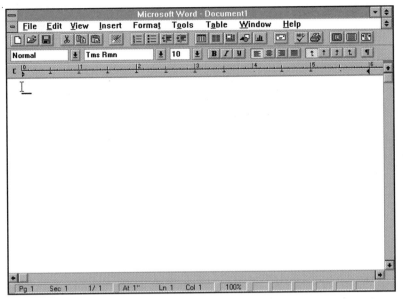

after

5. Double-click on the program icon for Word for Windows.

   This step starts the Word for Windows program. A blank document appears in a window on-screen. For information on the parts of the Word for Windows screen, see the Basics part of this book.

1. Turn on the computer and monitor.

2. Respond to the prompts for the date and time, if necessary.

3. Type **win** and press **Enter**.

4. Double-click on the group icon for Word for Windows.

5. Double-click on the program icon for Word for Windows.

Exit Word for Windows
To exit Word for Windows, see *TASK: Exit Word for Windows.*

To start Word for Windows

Program must be installed
To start Word for Windows, the program must be installed. Follow the installation procedures outlined in the Word for Windows manual.

Select a menu command

before

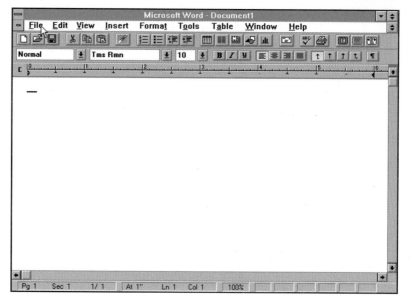

Oops!
To close a menu without
making a selection, click
on the menu name again
or press the Esc key.

1. Point to **File** in the menu bar and click the left mouse button.

   This step opens the menu. In this case, you are opening the File menu. You see a list of File commands.

2. Point to **Exit** and click the left mouse button.

   This step selects the command. In this case, you are selecting the Exit command. You return to the Microsoft Windows Program Manager.

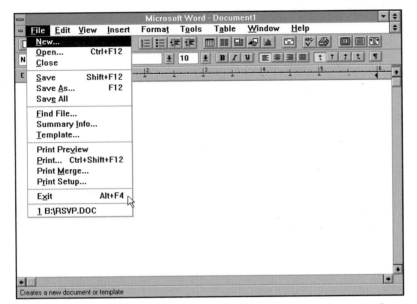

after

1. Click on the name of the menu you want to open.

2. Click on the command you want to execute.

To select a menu command

Commands with ellipses (...)
When you select a command followed by an ellipsis, Word for Windows displays a dialog box. The dialog box prompts you for additional information.

Use shortcut keys
If you prefer to keep your hands on the keyboard, learn the shortcut keys, which appear in the menus next to the command names. This book notes some shortcut keys in the exercises and in the *Quick Reference Guide*.

Exit Word for Windows

Oops!
To restart Word for Windows, see *TASK: Start Word for Windows.*

before

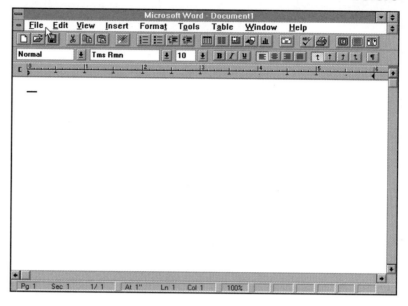

1. **Point to File in the menu bar and click the left mouse button.**

   This step opens the File menu. You see a list of File commands.

2. **Point to Exit and click the left mouse button.**

   This step selects the Exit command. You return to the Microsoft Windows Program Manager.

   Follow steps 3 through 5 to exit Microsoft Windows and return to DOS.

3. **In the Program Manager, point to File and click the left mouse button.**

   This step opens the Program Manager's File menu.

4. **Point to Exit Windows and click the left mouse button.**

   This step selects the Exit Windows command. You see the Exit Windows dialog box.

5. **Point to OK and click the left mouse button.**

   This step confirms that you do want to exit Microsoft Windows. You return to DOS and the prompt C:\> appears on-screen.

c:\>

after

Save the document
If you typed any text or made any changes to the document, Word for Windows prompts you to save the changes. See any of the tasks on saving a document in the Task/Review section *Managing Files.*

1. Click on **File** in the menu bar.

2. Click on the **Exit** command.

3. To exit Microsoft Windows, click on **File** in the Program Manager's menu bar.

4. Click on the **Exit Windows** command.

5. Click on **OK** or press **Enter**.

Keyboard shortcut
Press the Alt+F4 key combination to select the File Exit command.

Get help

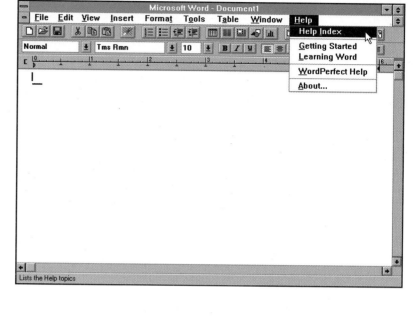

Oops!
To close the Help window, double-click on the Help window's Control menu box.

1. Point to **Help** in the menu bar and click the left mouse button.

   This step opens the Help menu. You see a list of Help commands (Help Index, Getting Started, Learning Word, and so on).

2. Point to **Help Index** and click the left mouse button.

   This step selects the Help Index command. Word for Windows opens the Help window. You see two groups of help topics: Step-by-step Instructions and Reference Information.

3. Point to **Alphabetic Listing** in the Step-by-step Instructions group and click the left mouse button.

   This step displays an alphabetical list of topics. When the mouse pointer is on a topic for which you can get help, the pointer changes to a hand with pointing finger.

4. Point to **Aligning text** and click the left mouse button.

   This step displays subtopics for the selected topic.

5. Point to **Centering text** and click the left mouse button.

   This step displays help on the selected topic. You see an explanation of how to center text. You can scroll this window by clicking on the scroll arrows. The After screen shows this step.

   After you read the explanation, close the Help window by following steps 5 and 6.

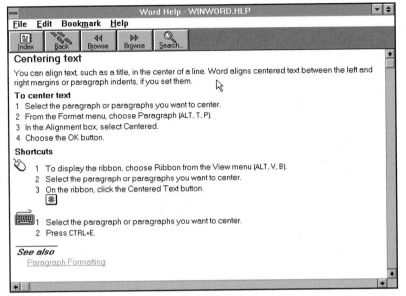

after

Need more help?
Word for Windows provides many ways to get help, and the Help feature has its own menu system. For complete information on all Help options, see *Using Word for Windows 2,* Special Edition (published by Que).

6. Point to **File** in the Help window's menu bar and click the left mouse button.

   This step opens the Help window's File menu. Be sure to click on the File menu within the Help window.

7. Point to **Exit** and click the left mouse button.

   This step selects the Exit command and closes the Help window.

REVIEW

1. Click on **Help** in the menu bar.

2. Click on the **Help Index** command.

3. Click on the type of listing you want to see.

4. Click on the topic you want to see.

5. Click on the subtopic you want to see.

6. To close the Help window, click on **File** in the Help window's menu bar.

7. Click on the **Exit** command.

To get help

Hide the Toolbar

before

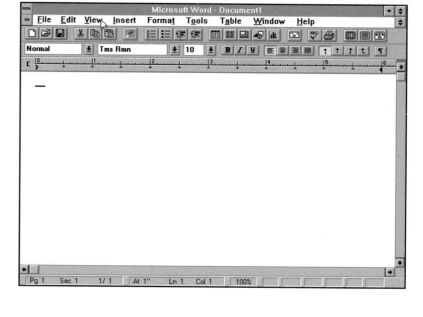

Oops!
The Toolbar command is a toggle. Select the Toolbar command again to display the Toolbar.

1. **Point to View in the menu bar and click the left mouse button.**

   This step opens the View menu. You see a list of View commands.

2. **Point to Toolbar and click the left mouse button.**

   This step selects the Toolbar command and hides the Toolbar (if the Toolbar appeared on-screen). If you select this command when the Toolbar is hidden, Word for Windows displays the Toolbar. For beginners, though, the screen may be less confusing with the Toolbar hidden. The screens in this book do not display the Toolbar.

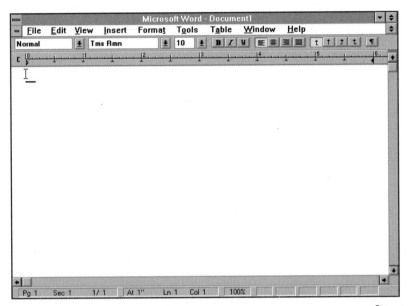

after

1. Click on **View** in the menu bar.

2. Click on the **Toolbar** command.

Use the Toolbar
You can use the Toolbar to select common menu commands quickly. For complete information on using the Toolbar, see *Using Word for Windows 2,* Special Edition.

To hide the Toolbar

Hide the ruler

before

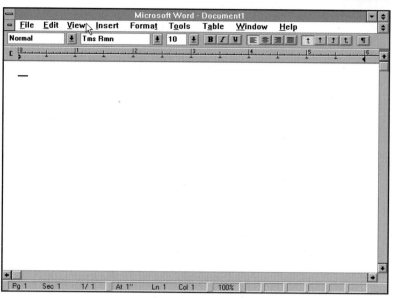

Oops!
The Ruler command is a toggle. Select the Ruler command again to display the ruler.

1. Point to **View** in the menu bar and click the left mouse button.

   This step opens the View menu. You see a list of View commands.

2. Point to **Ruler** and click the left mouse button.

   This step selects the Ruler command and hides the ruler (if the ruler appeared on-screen). If you select this command when the ruler is hidden, Word for Windows displays the ruler. For beginners, though, the screen may be less confusing with the ruler hidden. The screens in this book do not display the ruler.

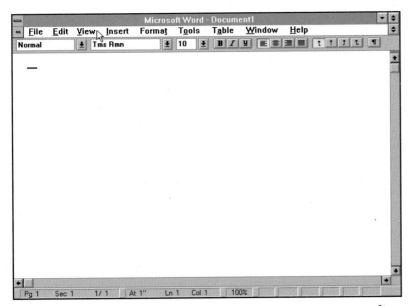

after

REVIEW

1. Click on **View** in the menu bar.

2. Click on the **Ruler** command.

To hide the ruler

Display
the ribbon

before

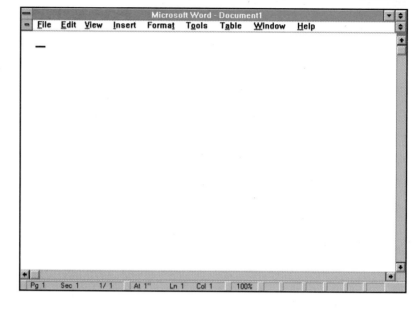

1. **Point to View in the menu bar and click the left mouse button.**

   This step opens the View menu. You see a list of View commands. If a check mark appears next to the Ribbon command, the ribbon is already on-screen. Follow these steps one time to hide the ribbon and then repeat the steps to display the ribbon again.

2. **Point to Ribbon and click the left mouse button.**

   This step selects the Ribbon command and displays the ribbon (if the ribbon was hidden). The screens in this book display the ribbon.

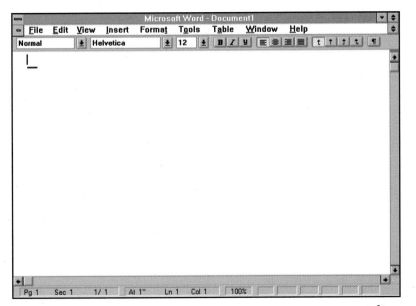

after

**Ribbon already
on-screen?**
If you select this
command when the
ribbon is on-screen, Word
for Windows hides the
ribbon.

1. Click on **View** in the menu bar.

2. Click on the **Ribbon** command.

To display
the ribbon

Use the ribbon
You can use the ribbon
to change the font and
alignment quickly. For
complete information
on using the ribbon,
see *Using Word for
Windows 2,* Special
Edition.

Add text

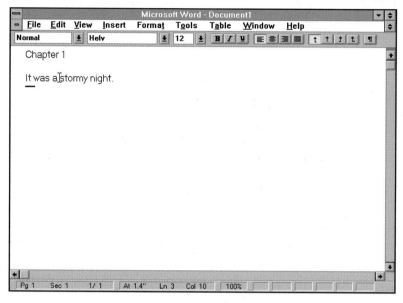

Oops!
To delete the text, select the Edit Undo Typing command immediately after typing the new text. Or, simply delete the text (see *TASK: Delete text*).

1. **Click before the word *stormy*.**

   This step places the insertion point where you want to insert text. You can place the insertion point by clicking the location or by using the arrow keys. (Remember, type the text in the Before screen before you start the exercise.)

2. **Type dark and.**

   This step inserts the new text you type and moves the existing text to the right.

3. **Press the space bar.**

   This step inserts a space between the new text and the original text.

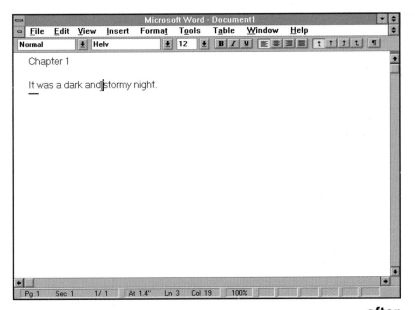

after

Overwrite text
Do not press the Ins key
to insert text. Pressing the
Ins key puts Word for
Windows in Overwrite
mode. See *TASK:
Overwrite text* for more
information.

REVIEW

1. Place the insertion point where you want to insert the new text.

2. Type the new text.

3. If necessary, type a space.

To add text

Overwrite text

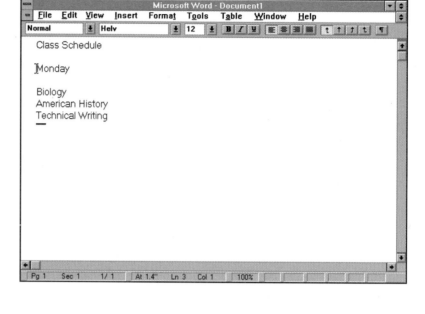

Oops!
To reverse the change, follow the same steps. You cannot undo overwritten text.

1. **Click before the *M* in *Monday*.**

   This step places the insertion point where you want to overwrite text. You can place the insertion point by clicking the location or by using the arrow keys. (Remember, type the text in the Before screen before you start the exercise.)

2. **Press Ins.**

   This step puts Word for Windows in Overwrite mode. The indicator OVR appears in the status bar at the bottom of the screen. This mode overwrites rather than inserts text.

3. **Type Fri.**

   Word for Windows deletes the original text (*Mon*) and replaces it with *Fri*.

4. **Press Ins.**

   The Ins key is a toggle. You press this key one time to turn on Overwrite mode. You press it again to turn off Overwrite mode.

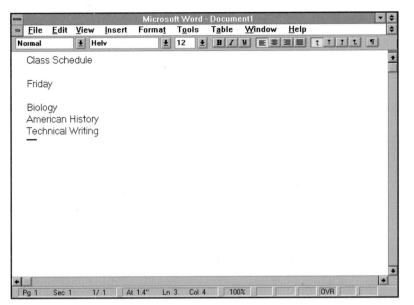

after

Use another method
You also can select the text you want to replace and start typing. The new text replaces all the selected text.

1. Place the insertion point where you want to start overwriting text.

2. Press **Ins** to turn on Overwrite mode.

3. Type the new text.

4. Press **Ins** again to turn off Overwrite mode.

To overwrite text

Insert a blank line

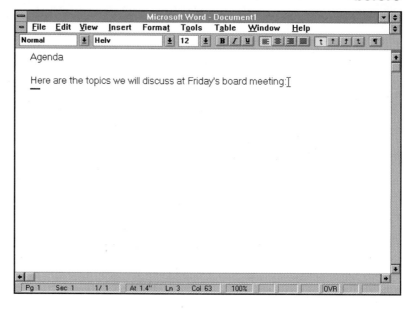

Oops!
To delete a blank line,
see *TASK: Combine
paragraphs.*

1. **Click after** *meeting:*.

   This step places the insertion point where you want to insert a blank line. Be sure to click after the colon at the end of the sentence.

2. **Press Enter.**

   Pressing Enter ends the current paragraph.

3. **Press Enter again.**

   This step inserts a blank line. When you press Enter, Word for Windows inserts a paragraph mark in the document. By default, paragraph marks (¶) do not appear on-screen. If you want to display paragraph marks, see *Using Word for Windows 2*, Special Edition.

4. **Type Scheduled projects.**

   The two lines of text are separated by a blank line.

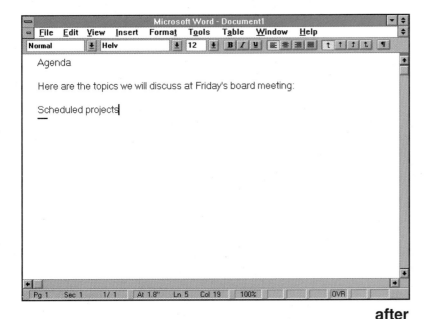

after

Word wrap
Unlike typing on a typewriter, you don't have to press Enter at the end of each line. When text reaches the end of the line, Word for Windows automatically wraps the text to the next line.

1. Place the insertion point where you want to insert a blank line.

2. Press **Enter** two times.

To insert a blank line

Hard return *v*. soft return
A hard return forces a line break. If you add or delete text, the hard return stays in the same position in the text. A soft return is inserted automatically by the program. When you add or delete text, the program adjusts the soft returns.

Entering and Editing Text

Combine paragraphs

before

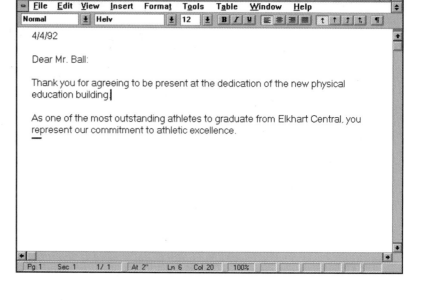

Oops!
To split the paragraphs, place the insertion point where you want the break to appear. Then press Enter two times.

1. Click after *building.* at the end of the first paragraph.

   This step places the insertion point at the end of the first paragraph. Be sure to click after the period.

2. **Press Del.**

   Pressing the Del key deletes the paragraph marker at the end of the current paragraph.

3. **Press Del again.**

   Pressing the Del key again deletes the blank line between the paragraphs. The second paragraph moves up next to the first paragraph.

4. **Press the space bar.**

   Pressing the space bar inserts a space between the two sentences.

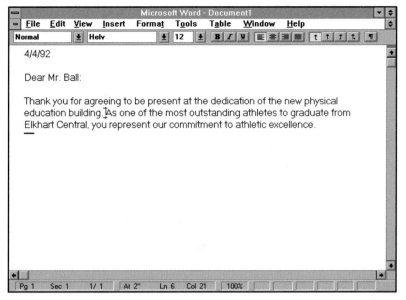

after

1. Place the insertion point at the end of the last line in the first paragraph.

2. Press **Del** two times.

3. Press the **space bar**.

To combine paragraphs

Insert a tab

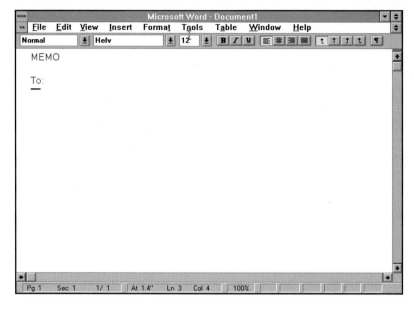

Oops!
To delete the tab, press
the Backspace key.

1. **Click after** *To:*.

    This step places the insertion point where you want to insert a tab. Be sure to click after the colon.

2. **Press Tab**.

    Pressing Tab inserts a tab and moves the insertion point to the next tab stop. Word for Windows provides a default tab stop every 1/2 inch. You also can change the tab settings (see *TASK: Set tabs*).

3. **Type All employees**.

    The text you type begins at the tab stop.

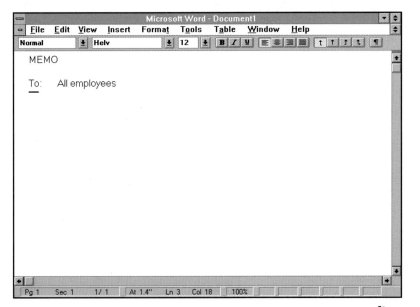

after

1. Place the insertion point where you want to insert the tab.

2. Press **Tab**.

Indent text
To indent an entire paragraph from the left margin, see *TASK: Indent text*.

To insert a tab

Display tab characters
When you press the Tab key, Word for Windows inserts a tab mark in the document. By default, tab marks (→) do not appear on-screen. If you want to display tab marks, see *Using Word for Windows 2*, Special Edition.

Enter a page break

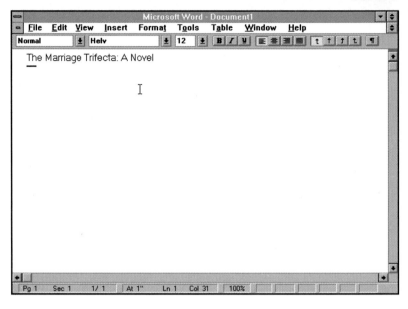

1. **Click after the word *Novel*.**

   This step places the insertion point where you want the new page to begin. Remember that you can place the insertion point by using the mouse or the arrow keys.

2. **Point to Insert in the menu bar and click the left mouse button.**

   This step opens the Insert menu. You see a list of Insert commands.

3. **Point to Break and click the left mouse button.**

   This step selects the Break command. You see the Break dialog box. The Page Break option button is selected by default.

4. **Click on OK.**

   This step inserts a page break in the document. A dotted line appears on-screen at that location. When you print the document, a new page will begin where you inserted the page break.

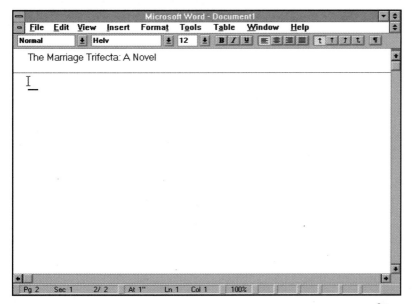

after

1. Place the insertion point where you want the new page to begin.

2. Click on **Insert** in the menu bar.

3. Click on the **Break** command.

4. Click on **OK**.

To enter a page break

What is a soft page break?
When the text reaches the end of a page, Word for Windows inserts a soft page break automatically. A soft page break appears as a dotted line on-screen (the dots are farther apart than those that indicate a hard page break). When you make changes, the program repaginates the document, adjusting the locations of the soft page breaks.

Entering and Editing Text

Go to a page

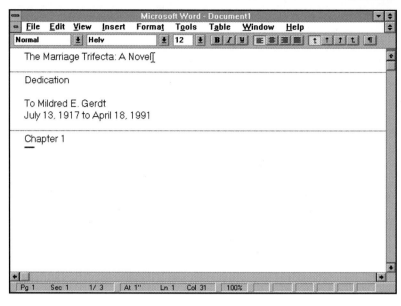

Oops!
To move back to the original page, follow the same procedure, but type the original page number.

1. **Click after the word** *Novel*.

   This step places the insertion point on page 1.

2. **Point to Edit in the menu bar and click the left mouse button.**

   This step opens the Edit menu. You see a list of Edit commands.

3. **Point to Go To and click the left mouse button..**

   This step selects the Go To command. You see the Go To dialog box. The insertion point is inside the Go To text box.

4. **Type 3.**

   Typing *3* tells Word for Windows to go to page 3.

5. **Click on OK.**

   This step confirms the command. Word for Windows moves the insertion point to page 3.

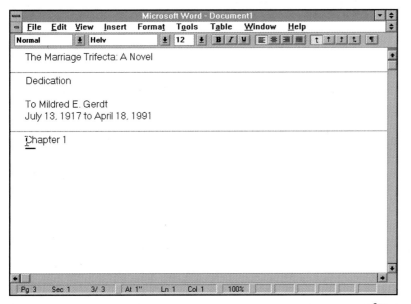

after

Go to the beginning or end of the document
To go to the beginning of the document, press the Ctrl+Home key combination. To go to the end of the document, press the Ctrl+End key combination.

R E V I E W

1. Click on **Edit** in the menu bar.

2. Click on the **Go To** command.

3. Type the page number.

4. Click on **OK**.

To go to a page

Keyboard shortcut
Press the F5 key two times to display the Go To dialog box.

Select text

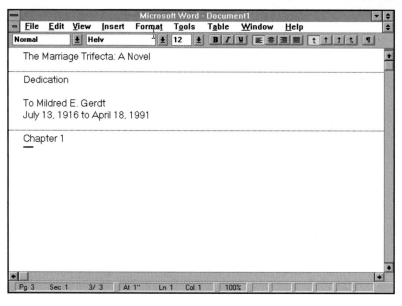

1. **Click before the *C* in *Chapter*.**

   This step places the insertion point where you want to start
   selecting text. You also can use the arrow keys to place the
   insertion point.

2. **Hold down the left mouse button and drag across the
   text until you highlight the entire line.**

   This step selects the text. As long as you hold down the mouse
   button, you can extend the selection.

3. **Release the mouse button.**

   The selected text remains in reverse video on-screen. After you
   select text, you can make many changes to the text—you can delete
   it, copy it, move it, make it bold, and so on. See the other tasks in
   this book.

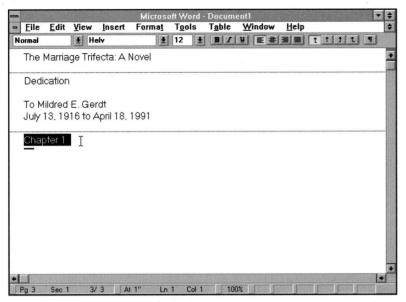

after

REVIEW

1. Click at the beginning of the text you want to select.

2. Hold down the left mouse button and drag across the text you want to select.

3. Release the mouse button.

To select text

Shortcuts
To select a word quickly, double-click the word. To select a sentence, hold down the Ctrl key and click the sentence. To select the entire document, select the Edit Select All command or press the Ctrl+5 key combination (using the 5 on the numeric keypad).

Delete text

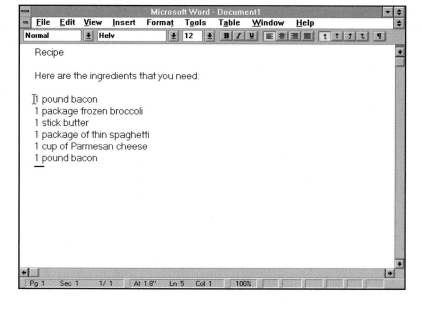

1. **Click before the *1* in the first line of ingredients (1 pound bacon).**

   This step places the insertion point before the text you want to delete. Be sure to place the insertion point at the beginning of the first occurrence of this text. (The text appears two times.)

2. **Select the words *1 pound bacon*.**

   You can use the mouse or the keyboard to select the text. To use the mouse, click at the beginning of the text, hold down the left mouse button, drag across the text you want to select, and then release the mouse button. To use the keyboard, place the insertion point at the beginning of the text, hold down the Shift key, use the arrow keys to select the text, and then release the Shift key. See *TASK: Select text* for more information. Be sure to select the entire line (the paragraph).

3. **Press Del.**

   Word for Windows deletes the text. The remaining text moves up (or over) to fill in the gap. (You also can press the Backspace key to delete the selected text.)

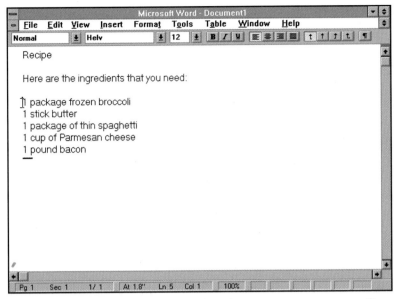

after

1. Select the text you want to delete.

2. Press **Del** or **Backspace**.

To delete text

Delete a character or a word
To delete just one character, use the Del or Backspace key. The Del key deletes the character to the right of the insertion point; the Backspace key deletes the character to the left of the insertion point. Press the Ctrl+Backspace key combination to delete the previous word; press the Ctrl+Del key combination to delete the next word.

Copy text

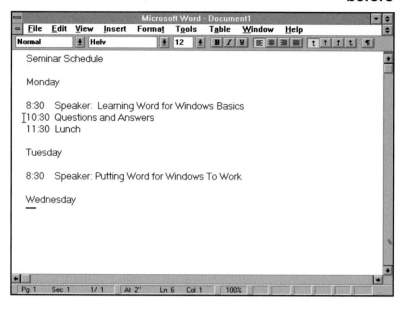

1. **Click before the *10* in *10:30*.**

   This step places the insertion point at the beginning of the text you want to copy.

2. **Select the next two lines (the line that begins with *10:30* and the line that begins with *11:30*).**

   You can use the mouse or the keyboard to select the text. To use the mouse, click at the beginning of the text, hold down the left mouse button, drag across the text you want to select, and then release the mouse button. To use the keyboard, place the insertion point at the beginning of the text, hold down the Shift key, use the arrow keys to select the text, and then release the Shift key. See *TASK: Select text* for more information.

3. **Point to Edit in the menu bar and click the left mouse button.**

   This step opens the Edit menu. You see a list of Edit commands.

4. **Point to Copy and click the left mouse button.**

   This step selects the Copy command. Word for Windows copies the text to the Clipboard. (The Clipboard is a temporary holding area for text and graphics.)

5. **Click on the blank line between *8:30* and *Wednesday*.**

   This step places the insertion point where you want the copied text to appear.

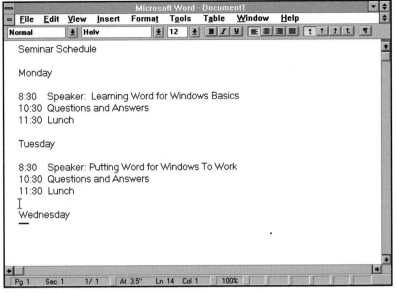

after

6. Point to **Edit** in the menu bar and click the left mouse button.

   This step opens the Edit menu again.

7. Point to **Paste** and click the left mouse button.

   This step selects the Paste command. The copied text now appears in the new location (as well as the original location).

1. Select the text you want to copy.

2. Click on **Edit** in the menu bar.

3. Click on the **Copy** command.

4. Place the insertion point where you want the copy of the text to appear.

5. Click on **Edit** in the menu bar.

6. Click on the **Paste** command.

Select, then do
Word for Windows follows the principle of select, then do. Before you can copy, move, or format text, you must select that text.

Keyboard shortcuts
Press the Ctrl+C or Ctrl+Ins key combination to select the Edit Copy command. Press the Ctrl+V or Shift+Ins key combination to select the Edit Paste command.

Move text

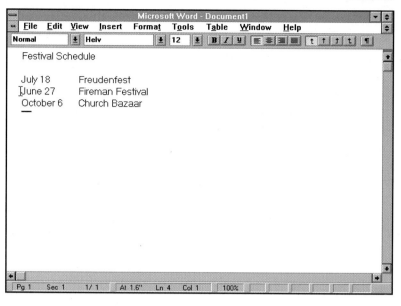

1. **Click before the *J* in *June*.**

   This step places the insertion point at the beginning of the text you want to move.

2. **Select the entire line.**

   You can use the mouse or the keyboard to select the text. To use the mouse, click at the beginning of the text, hold down the left mouse button, drag across the text you want to select, and then release the mouse button. To use the keyboard, place the insertion point at the beginning of the text, hold down the Shift key, use the arrow keys to select the text, and then release the Shift key. See *TASK: Select text* for more information.

   Be sure to select the entire line (the text and the hard return at the end of the line). The highlight should extend past the text into the margin.

3. **Point to Edit in the menu bar and click the left mouse button.**

   This step opens the Edit menu. You see a list of Edit commands.

4. **Point to Cut and click the left mouse button.**

   This step selects the Cut command. Word for Windows cuts the text from the document and places it on the Clipboard (a temporary holding area).

5. **Click before the *J* in *July*.**

   This step places the insertion point where you want to move the text.

Easy **Word for Windows**

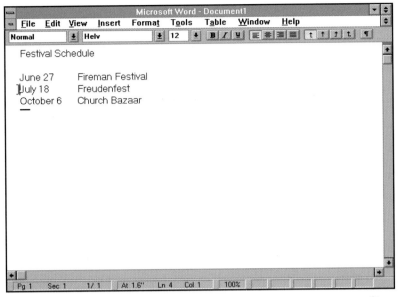

after

6. Point to **Edit** in the menu bar and click the left mouse button.

   This step opens the Edit menu again.

7. Point to **Paste** and click the left mouse button.

   This step selects the Paste command. The copied text now appears in the new location (but not in the original location).

1. Select the text you want to move.

2. Click on **Edit** in the menu bar.

3. Click on the **Cut** command.

4. Place the insertion point where you want the text to appear.

5. Click on **Edit** in the menu bar.

6. Click on the **Paste** command.

To move text

Select, then do
Word for Windows follows the principle of select, then do. Before you can copy, move, or format text, you must select that text.

Keyboard shortcuts
Press the Ctrl+X key combination to select the the Edit Cut command command. Press the Ctrl+V key combination to select the Edit Paste command.

Use Undo

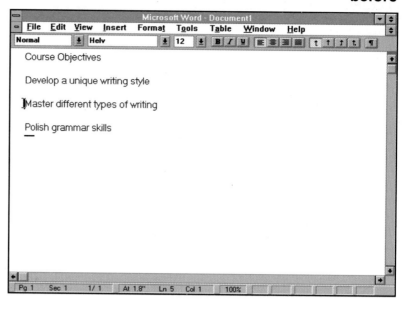

Oops!
Use the Edit Undo
Undo command to
undo the "undo."

1. **Click before the *M* in *Master*.**

   In this task, you will undo a text deletion. This step places the insertion point at the beginning of the text you will delete.

2. **Select the entire line and the following blank line.**

   You can use the mouse or the keyboard to select the text. To use the mouse, click at the beginning of the text, hold down the left mouse button, drag across the text you want to select, and then release the mouse button. To use the keyboard, place the insertion point at the beginning of the text, hold down the Shift key, use the arrow keys to select the text, and then release the Shift key. See *TASK: Select text* for more information.

3. **Press Del.**

   Word for Windows deletes the selected text.

4. **Point to Edit in the menu bar and click the left mouse button.**

   This step opens the Edit menu. You see a list of Edit commands.

5. **Point to Undo Edit Clear and click the left mouse button.**

   This step selects the Undo command. The deleted text is restored; the text remains selected.

Easy **Word for Windows**

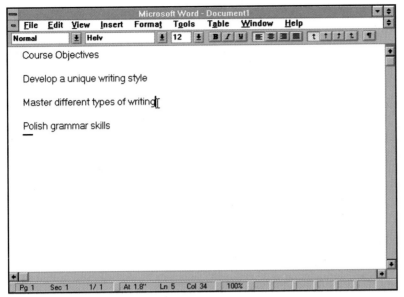

after

You can use the Undo command for other changes besides restoring deleted text. You can undo copying, moving, formatting, and so on. You cannot undo a merge or scrolling the document. Note that the name of the Undo command changes depending on the last action you performed.

6. **Click anywhere outside the text.**

   This step deselects the text. Note that the Before and After screens are the same.

Keyboard shortcut
Press the Ctrl+Z key combination to select the Edit Undo command.

1. Click on **Edit** in the menu bar.

2. Click on the **Undo** command.

To use Undo

Select Undo immediately
Undo reverses the *last* change you made to the document. If you make a change you want to undo, select the Edit Undo command immediately.

Managing Files

This section covers the following tasks:

Save a document for the first time

Save a document again

Save a document with a new name

Save and close a document

Create a new document

Open an existing document

Abandon changes

Open more than one document

Make a different document active

Display more than one document

Delete a document

Easy **Word for Windows**

Save a document for the first time

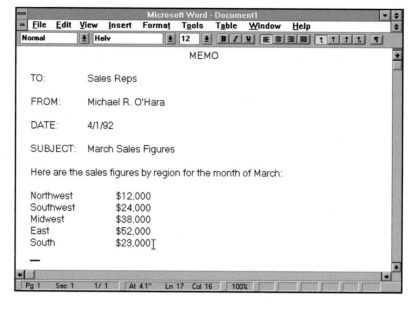

1. **Click on File in the menu bar.**

   This step opens the File menu. You see a list of File commands.

2. **Click on Save.**

   This step selects the Save command. The first time you save the file, you see the Save As dialog box. The insertion point is in the File Name text box so that you can type a file name.

   The Save As dialog box also contains a file list box, a directory list box, a drive drop-down list box, and a file type drop-down list box. For information on the other dialog box options, see *Using Word for Windows 2,* Special Edition.

3. **Type SALES.**

   SALES is the file name you want to assign to the document. Word for Windows automatically assigns the extension DOC.

   A file name consists of two parts: the root name and the extension. You can type up to eight characters for the root name. The extension, which can be up to three characters, usually indicates the type of file and is optional. A period separates the root name and the extension. As a general rule, use only letters and numbers for file names.

4. **Click on OK.**

   This step confirms the file name. By default, you see the Summary Info dialog box. In this dialog box, you can specify some additional information about the file. For information on using this dialog box, see *Using Word for Windows 2,* Special Edition. If you don't see the Summary Info dialog box, skip step 5.

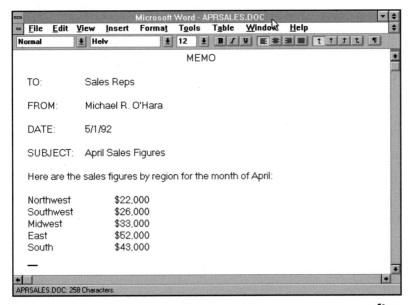

after

Save often
As a general rule, save every 5 to 15 minutes and before you try any task about which you are uncertain. To save the file again, see *TASK: Save a document again.*

5. Click on **OK**.

   This step closes the Summary Info dialog box without specifying any additional information about the file. Word for Windows saves the file to disk, and the document remains on-screen. The name of the file now appears in the title bar at the top of the screen.

REVIEW

1. Click on **File** in the menu bar.

2. Click on the **Save** command.

3. Type a file name.

4. Click on **OK**.

5. If the Summary Info dialog box appears, type any additional information about the file.

6. Click on **OK**.

To save a document for the first time

Keyboard shortcut
Press the Shift+F12 key combination to select the File Save command.

Save a document again

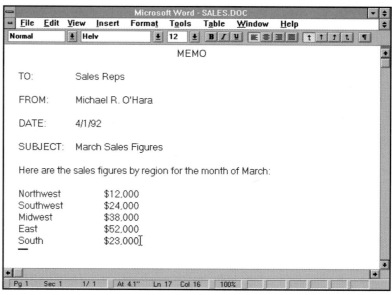

before

Oops!
If you don't want to save the file, you can abandon any changes you made. See *TASK: Abandon changes.*

1. **Click on File in the menu bar.**

   This step opens the File menu. You see a list of File commands.

2. **Click on Save.**

   This step selects the Save command. Word for Windows saves the file with the same file name, and the document remains on-screen.

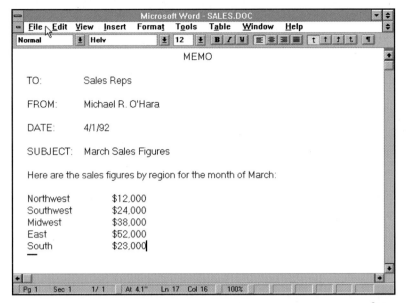

after

1. Click on **File** in the menu bar.

2. Click on the **Save** command.

To save a document again

Keyboard shortcut
Press the Shift+F12 key combination to select the File Save command.

Save a document with a new name

before

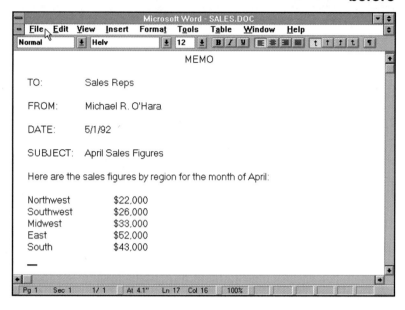

If you don't want to save the file, click on Cancel in step 4.

1. **Click on File in the menu bar.**

   This step opens the File menu. You see a list of File commands.

2. **Click on Save As.**

   This step selects the Save As command. You see the Save As dialog box. The insertion point is in the File Name text box so that you can type a file name.

   The Save As dialog box also contains a file list box, a directory list box, a drive drop-down list box, and a file type drop-down list box. For information on the other dialog box options, see *Using Word for Windows 2,* Special Edition.

3. **Type APRSALES.**

   APRSALES is the new file name you want to assign to the document. Word for Windows adds the DOC extension automatically.

4. **Click on OK.**

   This step confirms the file name. By default, you see the Summary Info dialog box. In this dialog box, you can specify some additional information about the file. For information on using this dialog box, see *Using Word for Windows 2,* Special Edition. If you don't see the Summary Info dialog box, skip step 5.

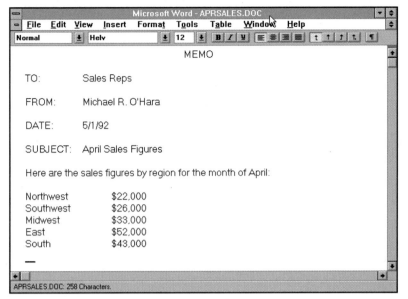

after

5. Click on **OK**.

This step closes the Summary Info dialog box without specifying any additional information about the file. Word for Windows saves the file to disk, and the document remains on-screen. The new file name now appears in the title bar. The original document is closed and remains intact on disk.

1. Click on **File** in the menu bar.

2. Click on the **Save As** command.

3. Type a file name.

4. Click on **OK**.

5. If the Summary Info dialog box appears, type any additional information about the file.

6. Click on **OK**.

To save a document with a new name

Type the name of another file?
If you type the same name as another file, an alert box asks Do you want to replace the existing *filename*? (where *filename* is the name of the file). Click on No and type a different name.

Keyboard shortcut
Press the F12 key to select the File Save As command.

Save and close a document

Oops!
To reopen the file, see
*TASK: Open an existing
document.*

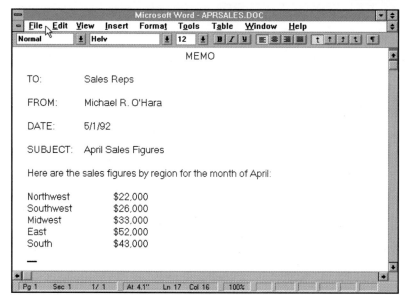

before

1. **Save the document.**

   For help with this step, see any of the tasks on saving a document. For this task, save the document shown in the Before screen as APRSALES.

2. **Click on File in the menu bar.**

   This step opens the File menu. You see a list of File commands.

3. **Click on Close.**

   This step selects the Close command. Word for Windows closes the document. If any other document windows are open, you see another document. Otherwise, you see only two menu names: File and Help. You can open an existing file or create a new file by selecting a command from the File menu. See *TASK: Open an existing document* or *TASK: Create a new document*.

   If you made any changes but did not save the document, an alert box asks Do you want to save changes to *filename*? (where *filename* is the name of the file). Click on Yes to save and close the document; click on No to close the document without saving the changes.

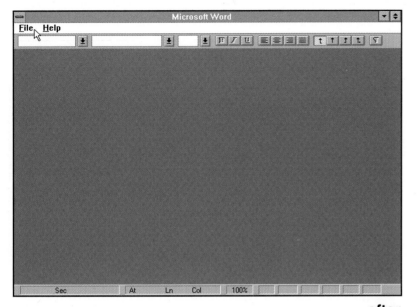

after

Why close documents?
You should close all
documents that you are
not working on to save
memory and to speed
performance.

1. Save the document.

2. Click on **File** in the menu bar.

3. Click on the **Close** command.

To save and close a document

Create a new document

Oops!
If you don't want to create a new document, abandon the new document. See *TASK: Abandon changes.*

before

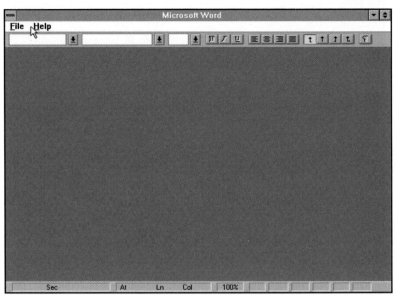

1. **Click on File in the menu bar.**

   This step opens the File menu. You see a list of File commands.

2. **Click on New.**

   This step selects the New command. You see the New dialog box. In this dialog box, you can select a template (a predesigned document) on which to base the new document. The default template is NORMAL. See *Using Word for Windows 2,* Special Edition, for complete information on templates.

3. **Click on OK.**

   This step tells Word for Windows to base the new document on the NORMAL template. A new document appears on-screen. Document2 appears in the title bar. (The number in the document name depends on how many unsaved documents you have open.)

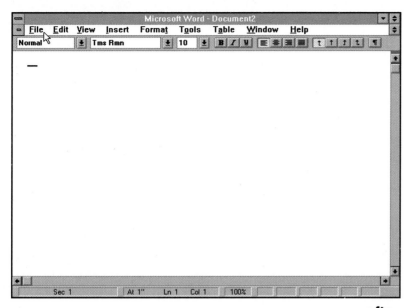

after

1. Click on **File** in the menu bar.

2. Click on the **New** command.

3. Click on **OK**.

**To create
a new
document**

Open an existing document

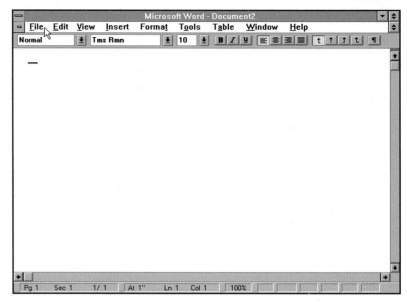

Oops!
If you don't want to open the file, click on Cancel in step 4.

1. **Click on File in the menu bar.**

   This step opens the File menu. You see a list of File commands.

2. **Click on Open.**

   This step selects the Open command. You see the Open dialog box. The insertion point is in the File Name text box so that you can type a file name.

   The Open dialog box also contains a file list box, a directory list box, and other options. By default, Word for Windows lists only DOC files; if a file has a different extension, you won't see its name in the file list. See *Using Word for Windows 2*, Special Edition, for information on how to display other files types and how to change drives or directories.

3. **Type APRSALES.**

   APRSALES is the name of the file you want to open. You can type the name or click on the name in the file list.

4. **Click on OK.**

   This step selects the OK button; the document appears on-screen. You see the file name in the title bar.

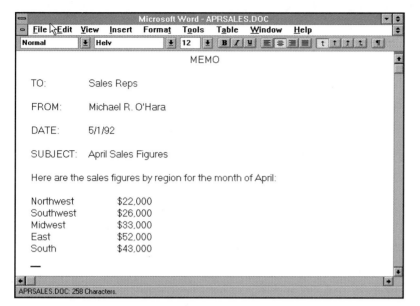

after

File not found?
If a message box tells you This document does not exist, click on OK and double-check that you typed the correct file name.

1. Click on **File** in the menu bar.

2. Click on the **Open** command.

3. Type or click on the name of the file you want to open.

4. Click on **OK**.

To open an existing document

Shortcuts
Press the Ctrl+F12 key combination to select the File Open command. Or, to reopen one of the last four files you opened, simply click on its name at the bottom of the File menu.

Abandon changes

before

```
─ Microsoft Word - APRSALES.DOC          ▼ ▲
─ File  Edit  View  Insert  Format  Tools  Table  Window  Help          ▲
 Normal    ± Helv        ± 12 ±  B I U  ≡ ≢ ≡ ≡  ↑ ↑ ↑ ↑  ¶
                        MEMO                                              ▲

        TO:        Sales Reps

        FROM:      Michael R. O'Hara

        DATE:      5/1/92

        SUBJECT:   April Sales Figures

        Here are the sales figures by region for the month of April:

        Northwest      $22,000
        Southwest      $26,000
        Midwest        $33,000
        East           $52,000
        South          $43,000
        |
                                                                         ▼
 Pg 1    Sec 1     1/ 1    At 4.3"   Ln 18  Col 1      100%
```

Oops!

If you want to save your changes, click on Yes in step 3; Word for Windows saves and closes the document. If you want to return to the document, click on Cancel in step 3.

1. **Click on File in the menu bar.**

   This step opens the File menu. You see a list of File commands.

2. **Click on Close.**

   This step selects the Close command. If you made any changes to the document, you see an alert box that asks Do you want to save changes to *filename*? (where *filename* is the name of the file).

   If you did not make any changes, Word for Windows closes the document, and you skip step 3.

3. **Click on No.**

   This step closes the document; any changes you made are lost. If any other document windows are open, you see another document. Otherwise, you see only two menu names: File and Help. You can open an existing file or create a new file by selecting a command from the File menu. See *TASK: Open an existing document* or *TASK: Create a new document*.

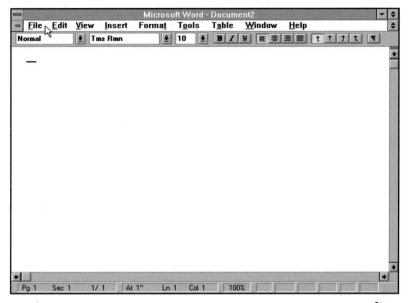

after

1. Click on **File** in the menu bar.

2. Click on the **Close** command.

3. If necessary, click on **No**.

To abandon changes

Open more than one document

before

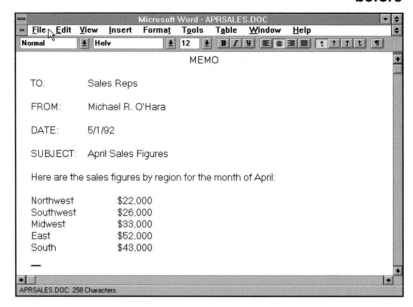

Oops!
To close a document, see
*TASK: Save and close a
document.*

1. **Click on File in the menu bar.**

   This step opens the File menu. You see a list of File commands.

2. **Click on Open.**

   This step selects the Open command. You see the Open dialog box. The insertion point is in the File Name text box.

3. **Type APRSALES.**

   APRSALES is the name of the first file you want to open.

4. **Click on OK.**

   This step confirms the command. The file you selected appears on-screen.

   Follow steps 5 through 8 to open another document.

5. **Click on File in the menu bar.**

6. **Click on Open.**

7. **Type SALES.**

   SALES is the name of the second file you want to open.

8. **Click on OK.**

   This step selects the OK button. The document appears on-screen on top of the first document you opened. The first document is still open, but you can't see it—you see only the most recently opened document. To display both documents, see *TASK: Display more than one document.*

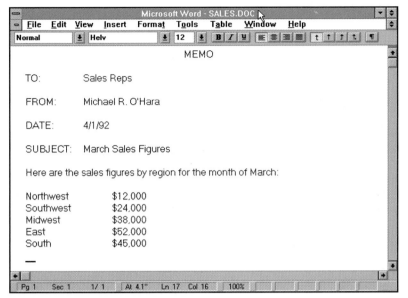

after

With both documents open, you can copy text from one document to the other, compare documents, and display both documents.

Document limit
Depending on the amount of memory you have, you can open up to nine documents.

REVIEW

To open more than one document

1. Click on **File** in the menu bar.

2. Click on the **Open** command.

3. Type or click on the name of the first file you want to open.

4. Click on **OK**.

5. To open the next file, click on **File** in the menu bar.

6. Click on the **Open** command.

7. Type or click on the name of the next file you want to open.

8. Click on **OK**.

Make a different document active

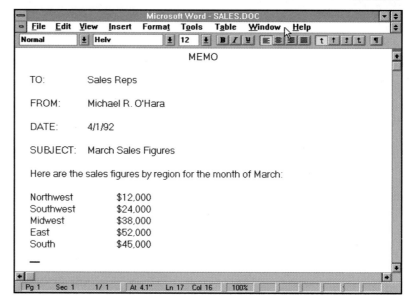

Oops!
Follow the same procedure to switch to a different document.

1. **Open the documents with which you want to work.**

   For help with this step, see *TASK: Open more than one document*. The example uses the documents SALES.DOC and APRSALES.DOC. If you don't have these documents, open two documents you do have. The document that you opened last is the current or active document—in this case, APRSALES.DOC.

2. **Click on Window in the menu bar.**

   This step opens the Window menu. You see a list of Window commands. Note that at the bottom of this menu, Word for Windows lists the currently open documents.

3. **Click on SALES.DOC.**

   This step selects the SALES.DOC document; this document becomes the active (or current) document.

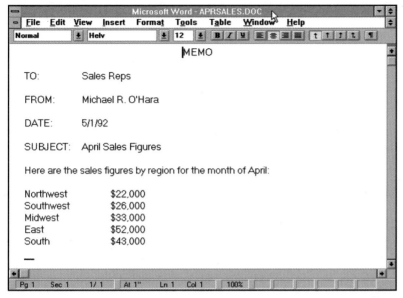

after

1. Open the documents with which you want to work.

2. Click on **Window** in the menu bar.

3. Click on the name of the document you want to make active.

To make a different document active

Shortcut
If you can see the document you want to make active, you can click within that document window to make the document active.

Display more than one document

before

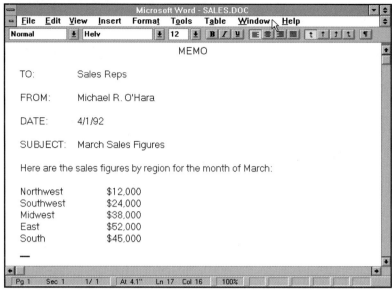

Oops!
To return a document to full-screen display, move to that document and then click on the up arrow in the title bar of its window (the Maximize icon) or double-click on that window's title bar. The window expands to fill the entire screen.

1. **Open the documents you want to display.**

   For help with this step, see *TASK: Open more than one document*. For this task, open SALES.DOC and APRSALES.DOC. If you don't have these two documents, open two documents you do have.

2. **Click on Window in the menu bar.**

   This step opens the Window menu. You see a list of Window commands.

3. **Click on Arrange All.**

   This step selects the Arrange All command. Each document appears in a separate window on-screen. The active, or current, document (the document that contains the insertion point) has a darker or colored title bar. Only one document can be active at one time.

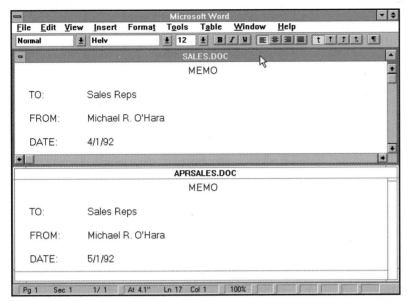

after

Move to a different document
To make a different document active, see *TASK: Make a different document active.*

1. Open the documents you want to display.

2. Click on **Window** in the menu bar.

3. Click on the **Arrange All** command.

To display more than one document

Delete a document

before

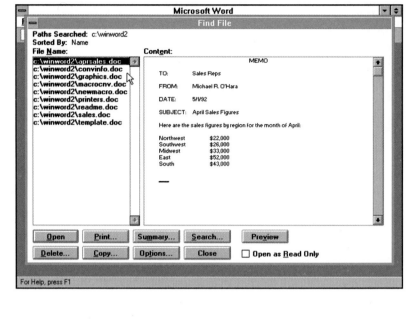

Oops!
If you change your mind,
click on Cancel in step 4
or step 5.

1. Click on **File** in the menu bar.

   This step opens the File menu. You see a list of File commands.

2. Click on **Find File**.

   This step selects the Find File command. You see the Find File dialog box. You can use this dialog box to delete files. You also can change the directories the program searches. (For information on other Find File options, see *Using Word for Windows 2,* Special Edition.) The Before screen shows this step.

3. In the file list, click on the file **SALES.DOC**.

   This step selects the file you want to delete. (If you don't have this file, select any file you don't need anymore.) You see the contents of that file in the Content area of the dialog box.

4. Click on **Delete**.

   This step selects the Delete button. You see an alert box asking you to confirm the deletion. (If the file is open, you can't delete it. In this case, you see an error message. Click on OK, close the document, and then try again.)

5. Click on **Yes**.

   This step deletes the file. The file no longer appears in the file list. The After screen shows this step.

6. Click on **Close**.

   This step closes the Find File dialog box.

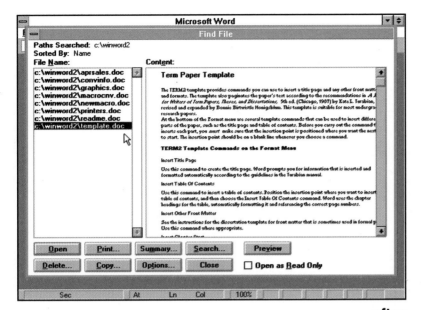

after

1. Click on **File** in the menu bar.

2. Click on the **Find File** command.

3. Click on the file you want to delete.

4. Click on the **Delete** button.

5. Click on **Yes**.

6. Click on the **Close** button.

Caution
Be careful when you delete files. Do not delete any files that you still need.

To delete a document

Other file management tasks
For information on other Find File options, see *Using Word for Windows 2,* Special Edition.

Formatting

This section covers the following tasks:

Boldface text

Italicize text

Underline text

Change the font

Change the font size

Center text

Align text flush right

Indent text

Create a hanging indent

Boldface text

before

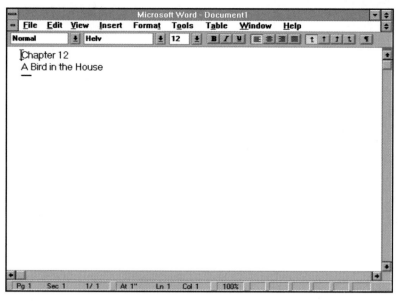

Oops!
To undo the formatting change, select the Edit Undo Formatting command immediately.

1. **Click before the *C* in *Chapter*.**

   This step places the insertion point at the beginning of the text you want to make bold.

2. **Select the next two lines.**

   You can use the mouse or the keyboard to select the text. To use the mouse, click at the beginning of the text, hold down the left mouse button, drag across the text you want to select, and then release the mouse button. To use the keyboard, place the insertion point at the beginning of the text, hold down the Shift key, use the arrow keys to select the text, and then release the Shift key. See *TASK: Select text* for more information.

   This task works on several lines. You can make any amount of text bold—just select the text you want to change.

3. **Click on Format in the menu bar.**

   This step opens the Format menu and displays the Format commands.

4. **Click on Character.**

   This step selects the Character command and displays the Character dialog box. This dialog box controls the font, size, style, color, position, and spacing of characters.

5. **In the Style area, click on Bold.**

   This step selects the Bold check box. In the dialog box, you see a sample of how the text will appear.

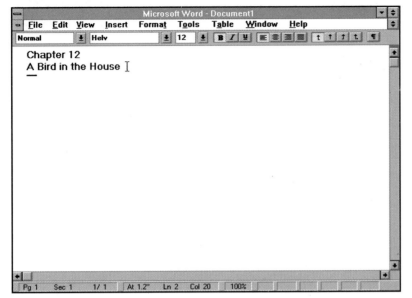

after

Shortcuts
Press the Ctrl+B key
combination to select the
Bold command. Or, click
on the B icon in the
ribbon to turn on bold
formatting.

6. Click on **OK**.

   This step confirms the choice and closes the dialog box. The
   selected text is now bold.

7. Click outside the selected text.

   This step deselects the text.

REVIEW

1. Select the text you want to make bold.

2. Click on **Format** in the menu bar.

3. Click on the **Character** command.

4. Click on **Bold**.

5. Click on **OK**.

6. Click outside the text.

To boldface text

**Turn on bold before
you type**
To turn on bold formatting
before you type, place the
insertion point where you
want to type bold text and
select the Bold command.
Type the text and then
select the Bold command
again to return to plain
formatting.

Italicize text

before

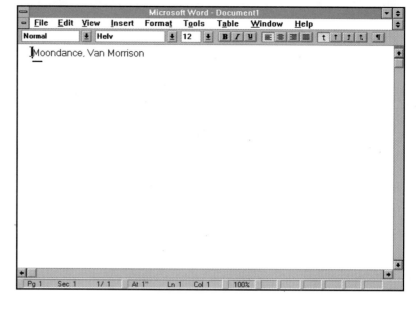

Oops!
To undo the formatting change, select the Edit Undo Formatting command immediately.

1. **Click before the *M* in *Moondance*.**

   This step places the insertion point at the beginning of the text you want to italicize.

2. **Select the word *Moondance*.**

   You can use the mouse or the keyboard to select the text. To use the mouse, click at the beginning of the text, hold down the left mouse button, drag across the text you want to select, and then release the mouse button. To use the keyboard, place the insertion point at the beginning of the text, hold down the Shift key, use the arrow keys to select the text, and then release the Shift key. See *TASK: Select text* for more information.

   This task works on one word. You can italicize any amount of text—just select the text you want to change.

3. **Click on Format in the menu bar.**

   This step opens the Format menu and displays the Format commands.

4. **Click on Character.**

   This step selects the Character command and displays the Character dialog box. This dialog box controls the font, size, style, color, position, and spacing of characters.

5. **In the Style area, click on Italic.**

   This step selects the Italic check box. In the dialog box, you see a sample of how the text will appear.

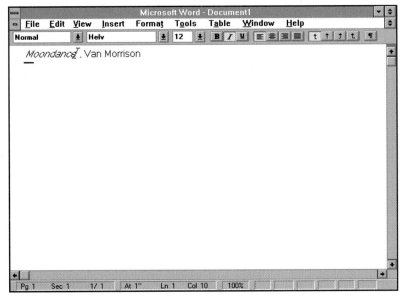

after

Shortcuts
Press the Ctrl+I key
combination to select the
Italic command. Or, click
on the I icon in the ribbon
to turn on Italic formatting.

6. Click on **OK**.

    This step confirms the choice and closes the dialog box. The
    selected text is now italic.

7. Click outside the selected text.

    This step deselects the text.

REVIEW

1. Select the text you want to italicize.

2. Click on **Format** in the menu bar.

3. Click on the **Character** command.

4. Click on **Italic**.

5. Click on **OK**.

6. Click outside the text.

To italicize text

**Turn on italic before
you type**
To turn on italic formatting
before you type, place the
insertion point where you
want to type italic text and
select the Italic command.
Type the text and then
select the Italic command
again to return to plain
formatting.

Underline text

before

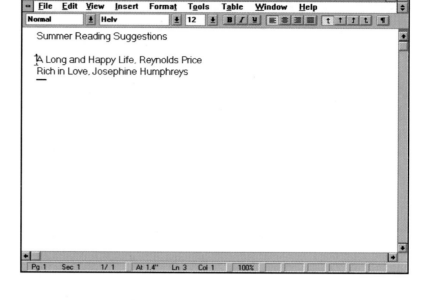

1. **Click before the *A* in *A Long and Happy Life*.**

   This step places the insertion point at the beginning of the text you want to underline.

2. **Select the text *A Long and Happy Life*.**

   You can use the mouse or the keyboard to select the text. To use the mouse, click at the beginning of the text, hold down the left mouse button, drag across the text you want to select, and then release the mouse button. To use the keyboard, place the insertion point at the beginning of the text, hold down the Shift key, use the arrow keys to select the text, and then release the Shift key. See *TASK: Select text* for more information.

   This task works on several words. You can underline any amount of text—just select the text you want to change.

3. **Click on Format in the menu bar.**

   This step opens the Format menu and displays the Format commands.

4. **Click on Character.**

   This step selects the Character command and displays the Character dialog box. This dialog box controls the font, size, style, color, position, and spacing of characters.

5. **Click on the down arrow at the end of the Underline drop-down list box.**

   This step displays a list of Underline choices.

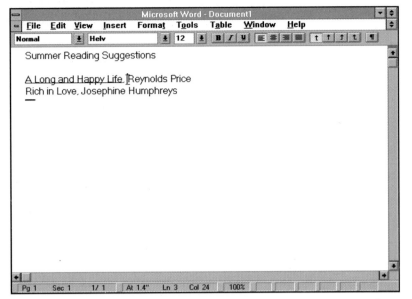

after

6. Click on **Single**.

This step selects Single underlining. In the dialog box, you see a sample of how the text will appear.

7. Click on **OK**.

This step confirms the choice and closes the dialog box. The selected text is now underlined.

8. Click outside the selected text.

This step deselects the text.

Shortcuts
Press the Ctrl+U key combination to select the Underline command. Or, click on the U icon in the ribbon to turn on Underline formatting.

Turn on underlining before you type
To turn on underlining before you type, place the insertion point where you want to type underlined text and select the Underline command. Type the text and then select the Underline command again to return to plain formatting.

REVIEW

1. Select the text you want to underline.

2. Click on **Format** in the menu bar.

3. Click on the **Character** command.

4. Click on the down arrow at the end of the Underline drop-down list box.

5. Click on the underlining style you want to use.

6. Click on **OK**.

7. Click outside the text.

To underline text

Formatting

Change the font

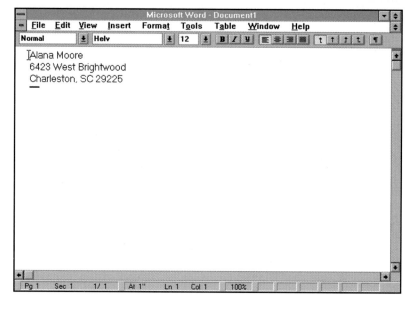

before

1. **Click before the *A* in *Alana*.**

   This step places the insertion point at the beginning of the text you want to change.

2. **Select the next three lines.**

   You can use the mouse or the keyboard to select the text. To use the mouse, click at the beginning of the text, hold down the left mouse button, drag across the text you want to select, and then release the mouse button. To use the keyboard, place the insertion point at the beginning of the text, hold down the Shift key, use the arrow keys to select the text, and then release the Shift key. See *TASK: Select text* for more information.

   This task works on several lines. You can change the font of any amount of text—just select the text you want to change.

3. **Click on Format in the menu bar.**

   This step opens the Format menu and displays the Format commands.

4. **Click on Character.**

   This step selects the Character command and displays the Character dialog box. This dialog box controls the font, size, style, color, position, and spacing of characters.

5. **Click on the down arrow at the end of the Font drop-down list box.**

   This step displays a drop-down list of fonts. The fonts you see depend on the printer you have selected.

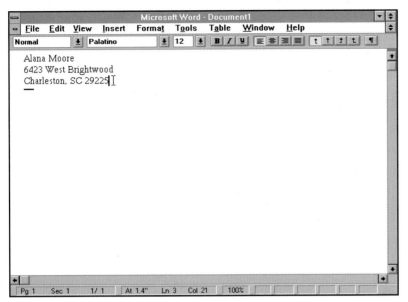

after

Use the ribbon
You also can use the ribbon to change the font. Click on the arrow next to the current font name and then click on the font you want to use.

6. Click on **Palatino**.

   If you don't have the Palatino font, select a font you do have. A sample of the new font appears in the lower right corner of the dialog box.

7. Click on **OK**.

   This step confirms the new font and closes the dialog box. The selected text now appears in the new font.

8. Click outside the selected text.

   This step deselects the text.

R E V I E W

To change the font

1. Select the text you want to change.

2. Click on **Format** in the menu bar.

3. Click on the **Character** command.

4. Click on the down arrow at the end of the Font drop-down list box.

5. In the font list, click on the font you want to use.

6. Click on **OK**.

7. Click outside the text.

Change the font size

before

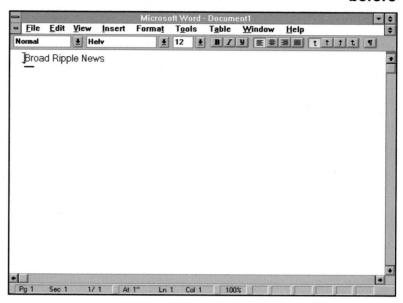

Oops!
To undo the formatting change, select the Edit Undo Formatting command immediately.

1. **Click before the *B* in *Broad*.**

   This step places the insertion point at the beginning of the text you want to change.

2. **Select the text *Broad Ripple News*.**

   You can use the mouse or the keyboard to select the text. To use the mouse, click at the beginning of the text, hold down the left mouse button, drag across the text you want to select, and then release the mouse button. To use the keyboard, place the insertion point at the beginning of the text, hold down the Shift key, use the arrow keys to select the text, and then release the Shift key. See *TASK: Select text* for more information.

   This task works on only one line. You can change any amount of text—just select the text you want to change.

3. **Click on Format in the menu bar.**

   This step opens the Format menu and displays the Format commands.

4. **Click on Character.**

   This step selects the Character command and displays the Character dialog box. This dialog box controls the font, size, style, color, position, and spacing of characters.

5. **Click on the down arrow at the end of the Points drop-down list box.**

   This step displays a drop-down list of available font sizes. Fonts are measured in points.

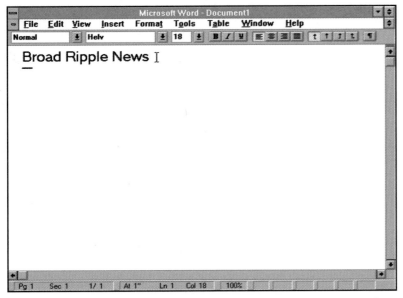

after

Use the ribbon
You also can use the ribbon to change the font size. Click on the arrow next to the current font size and then click on the font size you want to use.

6. In the font size list, click on **18**.

   This step selects 18-point type. If you don't have this font size, select a size you do have. A sample of the new font appears in the lower right corner of the dialog box.

7. Click on **OK**.

   This step confirms the new font size and closes the dialog box. The selected text now appears in the new font size.

8. Click outside the selected text.

   This step deselects the text.

REVIEW

To change the font size

1. Select the text you want to change.

2. Click on **Format** in the menu bar.

3. Click on the **Character** command.

4. Click on the down arrow at the end of the Points drop-down list box.

5. In the font size list, click on the font size you want to use.

6. Click on **OK**.

7. Click outside the text.

Center text

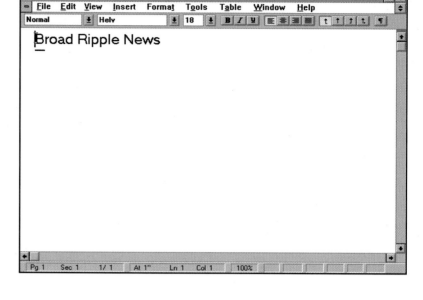

before

Oops!
To undo the formatting change, select the Edit Undo Formatting command immediately.

1. **Click before the *B* in *Broad Ripple News*.**

   This step places the insertion point at the beginning of the line you want to center.

2. **Click on Format in the menu bar.**

   This step opens the Format menu and displays the Format commands.

3. **Click on Paragraph.**

   This step selects the Paragraph command and displays the Paragraph dialog box. This dialog box controls the alignment, spacing, and pagination options for paragraphs.

4. **Click on the down arrow at the end of the Alignment drop-down list box.**

   This step displays a drop-down list of alignment choices.

5. **Click on Centered.**

   This step selects Centered alignment. You see a sample in the dialog box.

6. **Click on OK.**

   This step confirms the choice and closes the dialog box. The line is now centered.

7. **Click outside the selected text.**

   This step deselects the text.

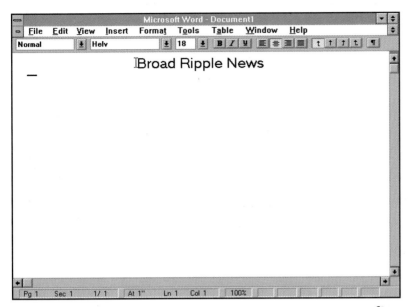

after

1. Place the insertion point at the beginning of the line you want to center.

2. Click on **Format** in the menu bar.

3. Click on the **Paragraph** command.

4. Click on the down arrow at the end of the Alignment drop-down list box.

5. Click on **Centered**.

6. Click on **OK**.

7. Click outside the text.

To center text

Center a line before you type
To center a line before you type, place the insertion point where you want to type centered text and select the Centered option. Then, type the text and press Enter.

Align text flush right

before

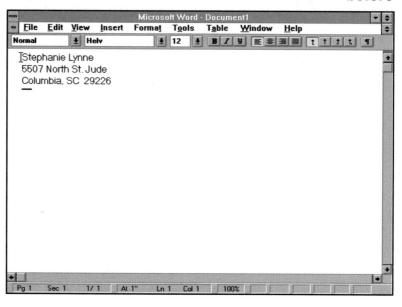

Oops!
To undo the formatting change, select the Edit Undo Formatting command immediately.

1. **Click before the _S_ in _Stephanie_.**

   This step places the insertion point at the beginning of the text you want to align.

2. **Select the next three lines.**

   You can use the mouse or the keyboard to select the text. To use the mouse, click at the beginning of the text, hold down the left mouse button, drag across the text you want to select, and then release the mouse button. To use the keyboard, place the insertion point at the beginning of the text, hold down the Shift key, use the arrow keys to select the text, and then release the Shift key. See _TASK: Select text_ for more information.

   This task aligns several paragraphs. You also can align one paragraph. To align only one paragraph, skip this step.

3. **Click on Format in the menu bar.**

   This step opens the Format menu and displays the Format commands.

4. **Click on Paragraph.**

   This step selects the Paragraph command and displays the Paragraph dialog box. This dialog box controls the alignment, spacing, and pagination options for paragraphs.

5. **Click on the down arrow at the end of the Alignment drop-down list box.**

   This step displays a drop-down list of alignment choices.

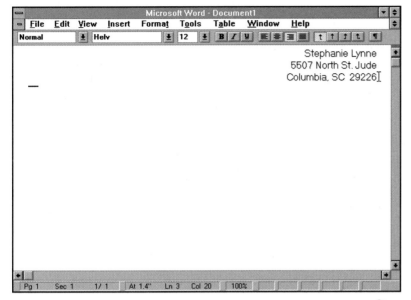

after

6. Click on **Right**.

   This step selects Right alignment. You see a sample in the dialog box.

7. Click on **OK**.

   This step confirms the choice and closes the dialog box. The lines are now right-justified.

8. Click outside the selected text.

   This step deselects the text.

To align text flush right

1. Place the insertion point at the beginning of the paragraph you want to align. To align several paragraphs, select those paragraphs.

2. Click on **Format** in the menu bar.

3. Click on the **Paragraph** command.

4. Click on the down arrow at the end of the Alignment drop-down list box.

5. Click on **Right**.

6. Click on **OK**.

7. Click outside the text.

Indent text

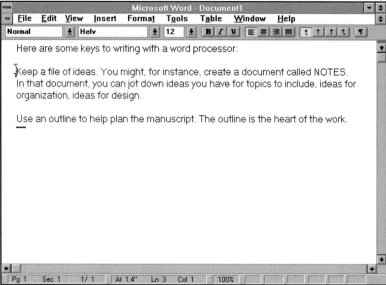

Here are some keys to writing with a word processor:

Keep a file of ideas. You might, for instance, create a document called NOTES. In that document, you can jot down ideas you have for topics to include, ideas for organization, ideas for design.

Use an outline to help plan the manuscript. The outline is the heart of the work.

Oops!
To undo the formatting change, select the Edit Undo Formatting command immediately.

1. **Click before the *K* in *Keep*.**

   This step places the insertion point where you want to indent text. This task indents one paragraph. You also can indent several paragraphs at one time. To indent more than one paragraph, select those paragraphs.

2. **Click on Format in the menu bar.**

   This step opens the Format menu and displays the Format commands.

3. **Click on Paragraph.**

   This step selects the Paragraph command and displays the Paragraph dialog box. This dialog box controls the alignment, spacing, and pagination options for paragraphs. The insertion point is in the From Left text box in the Indentation area.

4. **Type .25.**

   This step specifies a 1/4-inch indent.

5. **Click on OK.**

   This step confirms the choice and closes the dialog box. The paragraph is now indented.

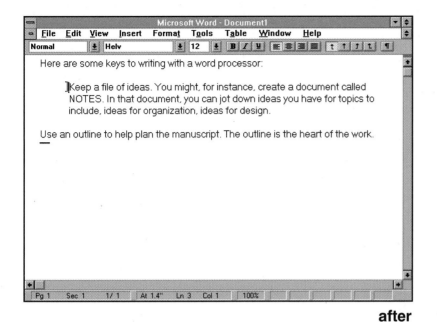

Here are some keys to writing with a word processor:

Keep a file of ideas. You might, for instance, create a document called NOTES. In that document, you can jot down ideas you have for topics to include, ideas for organization, ideas for design.

Use an outline to help plan the manuscript. The outline is the heart of the work.

after

Shortcuts
Press the Ctrl+N key combination to indent the current paragraph 1/4 inch. Press the Ctrl+M key combination to undo the indent.

REVIEW

1. Move the insertion point to the beginning of the paragraph you want to indent. To indent several paragraphs, select those paragraphs.

2. Click on **Format** in the menu bar.

3. Click on the **Paragraph** command.

4. In the From Left text box, type the amount you want to indent the text.

5. Click on **OK**.

To indent text

Create a hanging indent

before

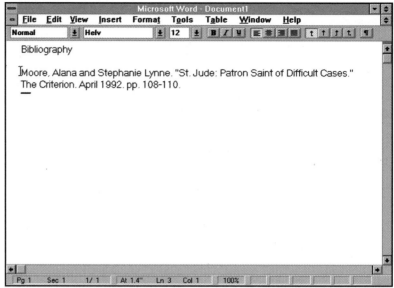

1. **Click before the *M* in *Moore*.**

   This step places the insertion point where you want to indent text. This task creates a hanging indent for one paragraph. You also can create hanging indents for several paragraphs at one time. To create hanging indents for more than one paragraph, select those paragraphs.

2. **Click on Format in the menu bar.**

   This step opens the Format menu and displays the Format commands.

3. **Click on Paragraph.**

   This step selects the Paragraph command and displays the Paragraph dialog box. This dialog box controls the alignment, spacing, and pagination options for paragraphs. The insertion point is in the From Left text box in the Indentation area.

4. **Type .5.**

   This step sets the amount of indentation for the paragraph. At this point, all lines will be indented .5 inch.

5. **Click in the First Line text box.**

   This step places the insertion point in the First Line text box. Here you type the amount of the indent for the first line of text.

6. **Type -.5.**

   This step tells Word for Windows to move the first line of text left .5 inch. This entry aligns the first line with the left margin. (Be sure to type the minus sign.)

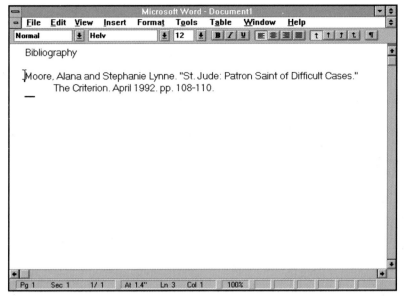

after

7. Click on **OK**.

   This step confirms the choice and closes the dialog box. The first line of the paragraph is flush left, but the second line is indented 1/2 inch.

REVIEW

To create a hanging indent

1. Move the insertion point to the beginning of the paragraph you want to indent. To indent several paragraphs, select those paragraphs.

2. Click on **Format** in the menu bar.

3. Click on the **Paragraph** command.

4. In the From Left text box, type the amount you want to indent the paragraph.

5. Click in the First Line text box.

6. Type the amount you want to move the first line of the paragraph to the left. Be sure to type a minus sign before the amount.

7. Click on **OK**.

Advanced Editing and Formatting

This section covers the following tasks:

Insert the date

Search for text

Replace text

Check spelling

Look up a word in the Thesaurus

Sort text

Set a default tab

Double-space a document

Set margins

Create a header

Edit a header

Create a footer

Edit a footer

Number pages

Add a border to a paragraph

Add a line to a paragraph

Easy **Word for Windows**

Insert the date

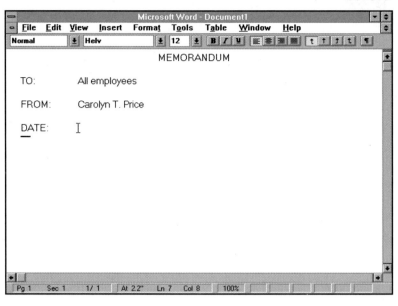

Oops!
To delete the date, select the Edit Undo Date Time command immediately after you insert the date.

1. **Click after *DATE:*.**

   This step places the insertion point. Be sure to click after the colon.

2. **Press Tab.**

   This step inserts a tab so that the text you type will align with the other entries. (Depending on your tab settings, you may have to press the Tab key two times.)

3. **Click on Insert.**

   This step opens the Insert menu. You see a list of Insert commands.

4. **Click on Date and Time.**

   This step selects the Date and Time command. You see the Date and Time dialog box. This dialog box lists the available date and time formats.

5. **Click on the third format—December 1, 1991.**

   This step selects the date format. You see the *current* date in the dialog box.

6. **Click on OK.**

   This step confirms the command. Word for Windows inserts a special code (called a *field code*) in the document, and you see the current date on-screen. For information on field codes (how to display and use them), see *Using Word for Windows 2,* Special Edition.

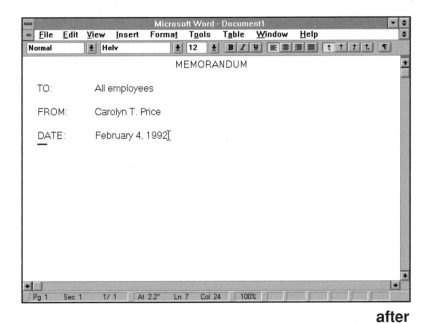

after

Delete the date later
When you insert the date, Word for Windows inserts a date code (which you do not see in normal view). If you try to back-space to delete the date, you hear a beep. To delete the date, you must select the entire date and then press the Del key.

1. Place the insertion point where you want to insert the date.

2. Click on **Insert** in the menu bar.

3. Click on the **Date and Time** command.

4. Click on the date format you want to use.

5. Click on **OK**.

To insert the date

Search for text

before

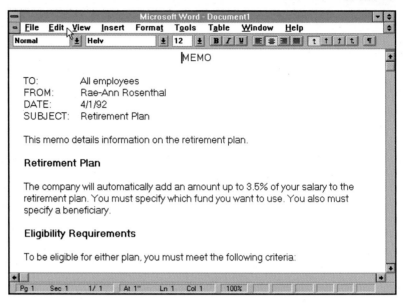

Oops!
If Word for Windows does not find the text, you see the message The search text is not found. Click on OK and try the search again. Be sure to type the search string correctly.

1. Press Ctrl+Home.

This step moves the insertion point to the beginning of the document. When you begin the search, Word for Windows searches from the location of the insertion point forward.

If you start searching when the insertion point is in the middle of the document, Word for Windows searches from that location to the end of the document and then displays a message box that asks whether you want to continue searching from the beginning.

2. Click on Edit.

This step opens the Edit menu. You see a list of Edit commands.

3. Click on Find.

This step selects the Find command. You see the Find dialog box. This dialog box includes the Find What text box and other options that control how the program searches the document. (See *Using Word for Windows 2,* Special Edition, for complete information on all the options.) The insertion point is in the Find What text box.

4. Type eligibility.

This text, called the *search string*, is what you want to find. You also can search for formatting. See *Using Word for Windows 2,* Special Edition, for information on this process.

By default, Word for Windows finds any occurrence of this text—regardless of the case. You can specify that you want to find only whole words and to match case. See *Using Word for Windows 2,* Special Edition, for complete information.

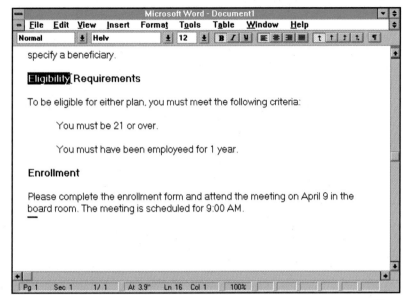

after

Search again
To search for the next occurrence of the search string, select the Find Next button again or press the Shift+F4 key combination instead of closing the dialog box.

5. Click on **Find Next**.

This step selects the Find Next button and starts the search. Word for Windows finds the first occurrence of the search string and selects that text. The dialog box remains open on-screen.

6. Click on **Cancel**.

This step selects the Cancel button and closes the dialog box.

REVIEW

To search for text

1. Press **Ctrl+Home** to move to the beginning of the document.

2. Click on **Edit** in the menu bar.

3. Click on the **Find** command.

4. Type the text you want to find.

5. Click on the **Find Next** button to start the search.

6. Click on **Cancel** to close the dialog box.

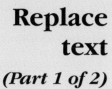

Replace text

(Part 1 of 2)

before

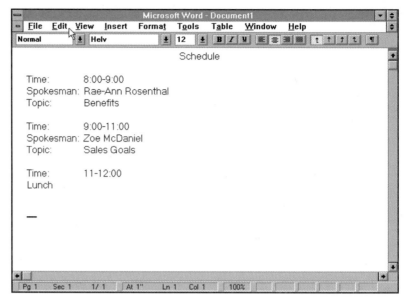

This task is split into two parts. These two pages contain the first part, Enter the search string. Turn the page for the second part, Replace the text.

Oops!
To cancel this procedure, click on the Cancel button.

1. **Press Ctrl+Home.**

   This step moves the insertion point to the beginning of the document. When you begin the search, Word for Windows searches from the location of the insertion point forward.

   If you start searching when the insertion point is in the middle of the document, Word for Windows searches from that location to the end of the document and then displays a message box that asks whether you want to continue searching from the beginning.

2. **Click on Edit.**

   This step opens the Edit menu. You see a list of Edit commands.

3. **Click on Replace.**

   This step selects the Replace command. You see the Replace dialog box. This dialog box includes the Find What text box, the Replace With text box, and other options that control how Word for Windows performs the search and replace operation. (See *Using Word for Windows 2*, Special Edition, for complete information on all the options.) The insertion point is in the Find What text box.

4. **Type Spokesman.**

   This text, called the *search string*, is what you want to find. You also can search for formatting. See *Using Word for Windows 2*, Special Edition, for information on this process.

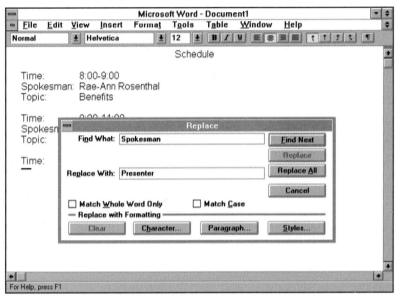

after

5. Click in the **Replace With** text box.

   This step places the insertion point in the Replace With text box so that you can type the replacement string.

6. Type **Presenter**.

   This is the text you want to use as the replacement.

1. Press **Ctrl+Home** to move to the beginning of the document.

2. Click on **Edit** in the menu bar.

3. Click on the **Replace** command.

4. Type the text you want to replace in the Find What text box.

5. Click in the **Replace With** text box.

6. Type the text you want to use as the replacement.

To replace text

Replace text
(Part 2 of 2)

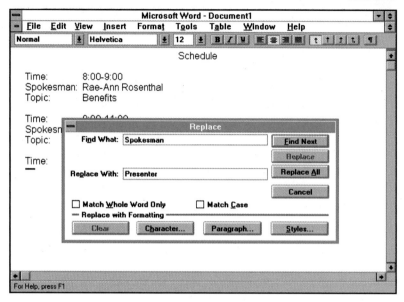

This task is split into two parts. The preceding two pages contain the first part, Enter the search string. These two pages contain the second part, Replace the text.

1. **Click on Find Next.**

   This step selects the Find Next button and starts the search. Word for Windows finds the first occurrence of the search string and selects that text. The dialog box remains open on-screen. (You can move the dialog box to see other text.)

2. **Click on Replace.**

   This step selects the Replace button. Word for Windows replaces the selected text with the new text and then moves to the next occurrence of the search string. The dialog box remains open on-screen.

3. **Click on Replace again.**

   This step selects the Replace button again. Word for Windows replaces the selected occurrence of the text and then moves to the next occurrence of the search string.

   When Word for Windows finds no more occurrences of the search string, nothing is selected in the document, and the Replace button is no longer available. The insertion point moves to the Find What text box to start another search and replace operation.

4. **Click on Close.**

   This step selects the Close button and closes the dialog box.

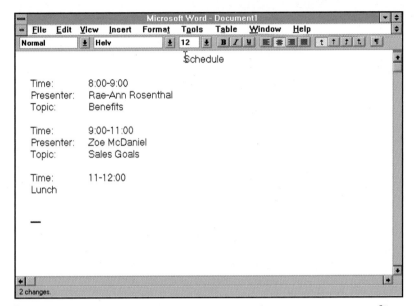

after

Replace all occurrences
To replace all occurrences of the text automatically, click on the Replace All button in step 7. (Before you make all the replacements, however, you may want to test the search and replace strings.)

1. Click on the **Find Next** button to start the search.

2. Click on the **Replace** button to make each replacement.

3. Click on **Close** to close the dialog box.

To replace text

Check spelling
(Part 1 of 2)

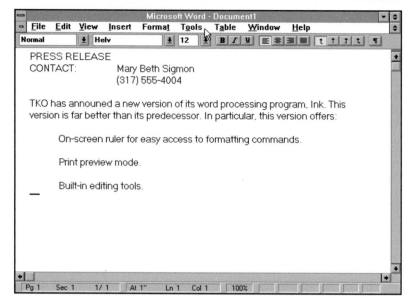

This task is split into two parts. These two pages contain the first part, Start the Speller. Turn the page for the second part, Correct the spelling.

Oops!
To stop the spell check, click on the Cancel button after Word for Windows stops on a word.

1. **Press Ctrl+Home.**

   This step moves the insertion point to the beginning of the document. When you begin the spell check, Word for Windows checks from the location of the insertion point forward.

   If you start the spell check when the insertion point is in the middle of the document, Word for Windows checks from that location to the end of the document and then displays a message box that asks whether you want to continue checking spelling from the beginning.

2. **Click on Tools.**

   This step opens the Tools menu. You see a list of Tools commands.

3. **Click on Spelling.**

   This step selects the Spelling command. Word for Windows begins checking the document. (If any text is selected, Word for Windows checks just the selected text.)

   The Speller compares the words in the document to the words in its dictionary and stops on words it cannot find. (This does not necessarily mean that the word is misspelled—only that Word for Windows' dictionary does not contain that word.)

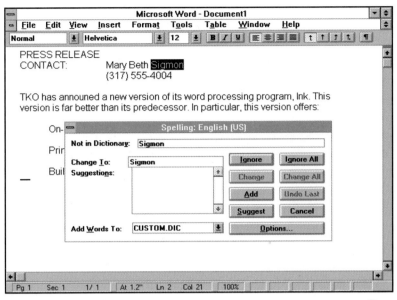

after

For this example, Word for Windows begins the spell check, stops on the word *Sigmon*, and displays the Spelling dialog box. This word appears in the Not in Dictionary box. Under the Not in Dictionary box, you see the Change To text box, which lists a suggested spelling. Beneath the Change To text box, you see additional suggestions. The Spelling dialog box includes buttons that enable you to ignore, ignore all, change, change all, or add the word to the dictionary.

1. Press **Ctrl+Home** to move to the beginning of the document.

2. Click on **Tools** in the menu bar.

3. Click on the **Spelling** command.

To check spelling

Check spelling
(Part 2 of 2)

before

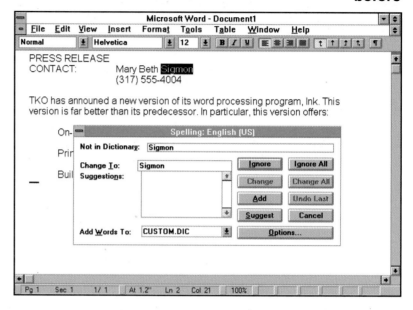

This task is split into two parts. The preceding two pages contain the first part, Start the Speller. These two pages contain the second part, Replace the text.

1. **Click on Ignore All.**

   This option tells Word for Windows to ignore all occurrences of this word (that is, not to stop on this word again). Word for Windows continues the spell check and stops on the word *announed*. The correct spelling—announced—appears in the Change To text box.

2. **Click on Change All.**

   This step replaces the incorrect spelling with the selected spelling. (If the correct spelling is not selected, click on the correct spelling in the suggestion list and then click on the Change or Change All button.)

   You see a message box that says the spell check is complete.

3. **Click on OK.**

   This step clears the message box.

Oops!
To stop the spell check, click on the Cancel button after Word for Windows stops on a word.

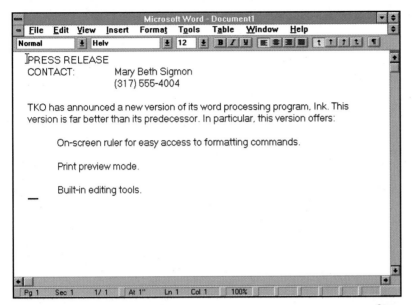

after

Use other options
Word for Windows offers many spell check options. For example, the Speller finds double words. You also can add words to the dictionary. For complete information, see *Using Word for Windows 2, Special Edition.*

REVIEW

1. When Word for Windows stops on a word, do one of the following:

   Select the **Ignore** button to ignore (skip) this occurrence of the word, but stop on the next one.

   Select the **Ignore All** button to ignore (skip) all occurrences of this word.

   Select the **Change** button to replace this occurrence of the word with the word in the Change To text box.

   Select the **Change All** button to replace all occurrences of the word with the word in the Change To text box.

   Select the **Add** button to add the word to the dictionary.

2. When you see the message that the spelling check is complete, click on **OK**.

To check spelling

Look up a word in the Thesaurus

before

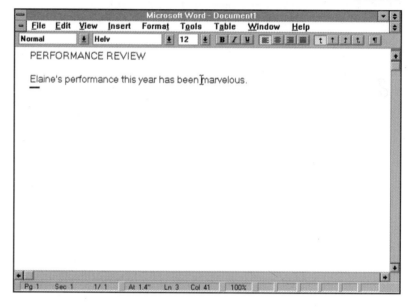

Oops!
To undo the replacement, select the Edit Undo Replace command immediately.

1. **Click before the word *marvelous*.**

   You can click before the word or within the word you want to look up.

2. **Click on Tools.**

   This step opens the Tools menu. You see a list of Tools commands.

3. **Click on Thesaurus.**

   This step selects the Thesaurus command. You see the Thesaurus dialog box. The Synonyms For box displays the selected word; beneath this box you see a list of meanings. To the right of the Synonyms For box, you see a list of synonyms; the first synonym is selected and appears in the Replace With text box.

4. **Click on outstanding.**

   This step selects the word outstanding in the Synonyms list box. The selected word appears in the Replace With text.

5. **Click on Replace.**

   This step selects the Replace button. Word for Windows replaces the original word (*marvelous*) with the new word (*outstanding*), and closes the dialog box.

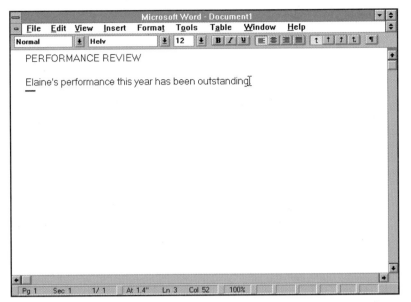

after

Keyboard shortcut
Press the Shift+F7 key
combination to select the
Thesaurus command.

To use the Thesaurus

1. Click before or within the word you want to look up.

2. Click on **Tools** in the menu bar.

3. Click on the **Thesaurus** command.

4. If you want to replace the original word, click on the word you want to use and then click on the **Replace** button.

Use other options
The Thesaurus feature
offers many options. For
example, you can display
additional synonyms.
For more information,
see *Using Word for
Windows 2,* Special
Edition.

Sort text

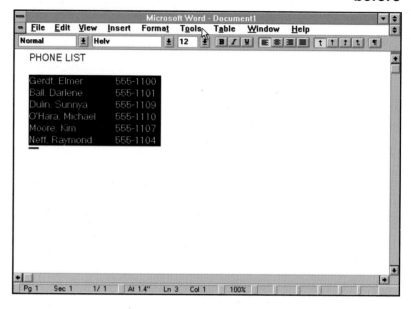

Oops!
To undo the sort, select
the Edit Undo Sorting
command immediately
after performing the sort.

1. Select the list of names and numbers.

You can use the mouse or the keyboard to select the text. To use
the mouse, click at the beginning of the text, hold down the left
mouse button, drag across the text you want to select, and then
release the mouse button. To use the keyboard, place the insertion
point at the beginning of the text, hold down the Shift key, use the
arrow keys to select the text, and then release the Shift key. See
TASK: Select text for more information.

Be sure to select just the list of names and numbers—don't select
the heading (Phone List). The Before screen shows this step.

2. Click on **Tools**.

This step opens the Tools menu. You see a list of Tools commands.

3. Click on **Sorting**.

This step selects the Sorting command. You see the Sorting dialog
box. The options in this dialog box control how Word for Windows
will perform the sort (the sorting order and the key fields). For this
task, the default settings are acceptable—that is, to sort the lines
alphabetically in ascending order by the first field. For complete
information on all the dialog box options, see *Using Word for
Windows 2,* Special Edition.

4. Click on **OK**.

This step selects the OK button. Word for Windows sorts the
selected text alphabetically, and the text remains selected.

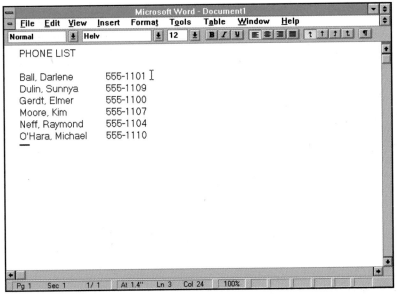

Save before sorting
Save the document before you sort so that you can abandon the sorted document and go back to the previous version if the sort doesn't work as planned.

after

5. Click outside the selected text.

This step deselects the text.

REVIEW

To sort text

1. Select the text you want to sort.

2. Click on **Tools** in the menu bar.

3. Click on the **Sorting** command.

4. If necessary, change any of the sort options.

5. Click on **OK**.

6. Click outside the selected text.

before

Set a default tab

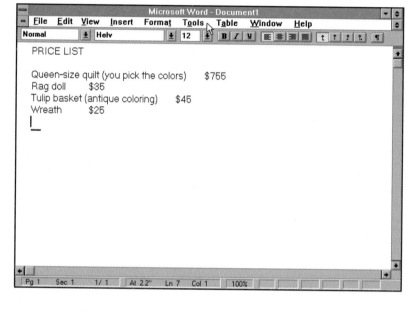

Oops!
Click Cancel in step 6 to cancel the changes.

1. **Click on** Format.

   This step opens the Format menu. You see a list of Format commands.

2. **Click on Tabs.**

   This step selects the Tabs command and displays the Tabs dialog box. In this dialog box, you can specify the position and the alignment of a tab. You also can add a leader (such as dots) before a tab. See *Using Word for Windows 2,* Special Edition, for complete information on all options.

3. **Click in the Default Tab Stops box.**

   This step moves the insertion point to the Default Tab Stops box. Because you want the tab to affect the entire document, you must set a default tab.

4. **Delete the current entry.**

   If the insertion point is before the current entry, press the Del key. If the insertion point is after the current entry, press the Backspace key.

5. **Type 3.**

   This step sets the location for the default tab. The default tab will be 3 inches from the left margin.

6. **Click on OK.**

   This step confirms the new tab setting and closes the dialog box. The default tab is now 3 inches from the left margin.

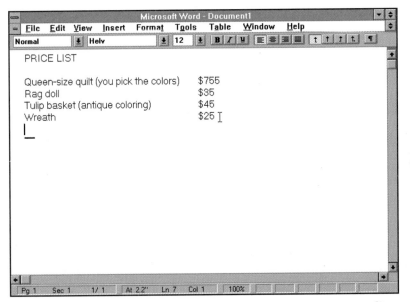

after

Tabs can be tricky
Setting tabs can be tricky. This procedure changes the tab stops for the entire document. You also can change the tab stops for just one paragraph. See *Using Word for Windows 2,* Special Edition, for complete information.

To set a default tab

1. Click on **Format** in the menu bar.

2. Click on the **Tabs** command.

3. Click in the **Default Tab Stops** text box.

4. Delete the current default tab.

5. Type the location of the tab you want to set.

6. Click on **OK**.

Use other tab types
You can choose different types of tab stops—right, decimal, or center tabs. You also can insert a dot leader before a tab stop. See *Using Word for Windows 2,* Special Edition, for more information on tabs.

Advanced Editing and Formatting

137

Double-space a document

before

```
Microsoft Word - Document1
File   Edit   View   Insert   Format   Tools   Table   Window   Help
Normal      Helv        12    B  I  U

Chapter 6
No Keepsies

        My family  always had their fingers in my love pie. Fixing this one up,
ruining that one. When I was seven, we went to Virginia Beach, and they tried to
pawn me off on some fat kid. My mom spotted him and thought it would be nice
if I played with him. This nice boy had a burr hair cut and looked like a Weeble.
Weebles wobble, but they don't fall down. Mom dubbed him Sluggo and invited
him to our hotel room to play. When he knocked on the door, I hid under the bed,
but my sister grabbed my ankles and pulled me out.
        Sluggo had just been to Williamsburg and had a bag full of marbles. He
said he'd teach me how to play, but he stressed we were playing for "no
keepsies." This meant that if I won and knocked the marbles out of the circle, I
couldn't keep them. As I slaughtered him at marbles, all Sluggo could say was,
"Remember, no keepsies. No keepsies." When I reported back to my mom about
the marble date, she got the biggest kick out of that phrase "no keepsies" that
she repeated "Sluggo" and "no keepsies" throughout the rest of the vacation—
actually, the rest of my life.

Pg 1    Sec 1    1/ 1    At 1"    Ln 1    Col 1    100%
```

Oops!

Click on Cancel in step 6 to close the dialog box without making a change.

1. **Select the entire document**

   To select the entire document, select the Edit Select All command or press the Ctrl+5 key combination (the 5 on the numeric keypad). Line spacing is a paragraph format; you can change the spacing for just one paragraph or for several paragraphs.

2. **Click on Format.**

   This step opens the Format menu. You see a list of Format commands.

3. **Click on Paragraph.**

   This step selects the Paragraph command and displays the Paragraph dialog box. In the Spacing area, note the Line Spacing drop-down list box.

4. **Click on the down arrow at the end of the Line Spacing drop-down list box.**

   This step displays a list of line spacing intervals.

5. **Click on Double.**

   This step tells Word for Windows to double-space the selected text (in this case, the entire document).

6. **Click on OK.**

   This step confirms the new spacing interval and double-spaces the text.

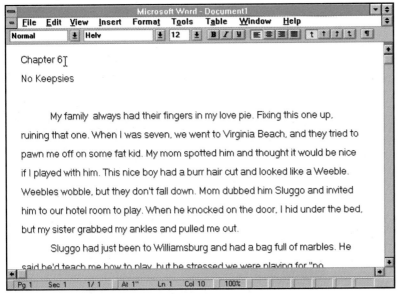

after

Revert to single spacing
To revert to single spacing, select the Edit Undo Formatting command immediately.

7. Click outside the selected text.

This step deselects the text.

1. Select the paragraphs that you want to double-space.

2. Click on **Format** in the menu bar.

3. Click on the **Paragraph** command.

4. Click on the down arrow at the end of the Line Spacing drop-down list box.

5. Click on the line spacing interval you want to use.

6. Click on **OK**.

7. Click outside the selected text.

To double-space a document

Set margins

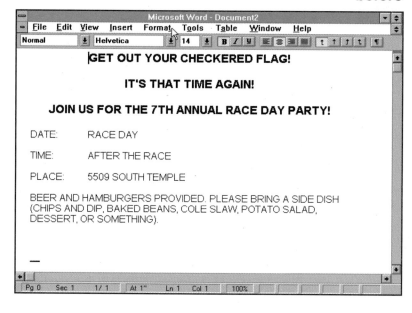

Oops!
To cancel the change,
click on Cancel in step 7
(in this *Task* section).

1. Click on **Format**.

   This step opens the Format menu. You see a list of Format commands.

2. Click on **Page Setup**.

   This step selects the Page Setup command and displays the Page Setup dialog box. You see text boxes for each of the four margins: Top, Bottom, Left, and Right. The default settings are as follows:

Top	1 inch
Bottom	1 inch
Left	1.25 inches
Right	1.25 inches

3. Click in the **Top** text box, press **Del** or **Backspace** to delete the current entry, and then type **2**.

   This step specifies a 2-inch top margin.

4. Click in the **Bottom** text box, press **Del** or **Backspace** to delete the current entry, and then type **2**.

   This step specifies a 2-inch bottom margin.

5. Click in the **Left** text box, press **Del** or **Backspace** to delete the current entry, and then type **2**.

   This step specifies a 2-inch left margin.

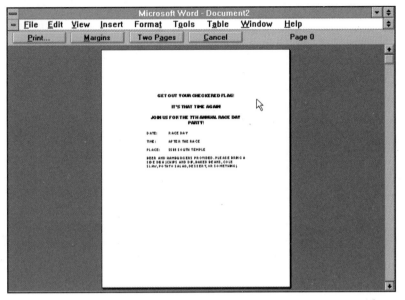

after

Default margins
To return to the default margins, select the Edit Undo Page Setup command immediately.

6. Click in the **Right** text box, press **Del** or **Backspace** to delete the current entry, and then type **2**.

   This step specifies a 2-inch right margin.

7. Click on **OK**.

   This step confirms the new margin settings and closes the dialog box. To see the effect of the margin changes, you must preview the document. See *TASK: Preview a document*. (The After screen shows a preview of the document.)

REVIEW

1. Click on **Format** in the menu bar.

2. Click on the **Page Setup** command.

3. Type the new margin setting in the appropriate text boxes (**Top**, **Bottom**, **Left**, or **Right**).

4. Click on **OK**.

To set margins

Create a header

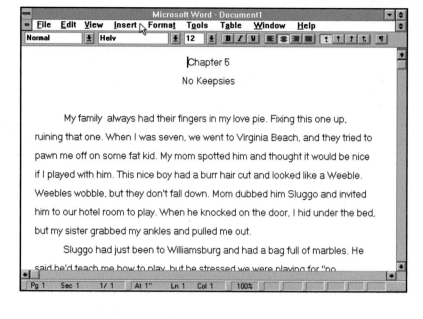

Oops!
To close the dialog box without creating a header, click on Cancel in step 4.

1. **Click on** View.

   This step opens the View menu. You see a list of View commands.

2. **Click on Header/Footer.**

   This step selects the Header/Footer command and displays the Header/Footer dialog box. You use the same dialog box to create headers or footers.

3. **Click on Header.**

   This step selects the Header option.

4. **Click on Different First Page so that the check box does not have an X in it.**

   By default, Word for Windows does not display a header on the first page of a document. This step turns off this option so that the header will appear on the first page.

5. **Click on OK.**

   In normal view, you see the Header window at the bottom of the screen. Even though the window is at the bottom of the screen, the header will print at the top of the page. You type the text of the header in this window. (You also can create headers in Page Layout view. See *Using Word for Windows 2*, Special Edition.)

6. **Type The Marriage Trifecta.**

   This is the text you want to print at the top of each page.

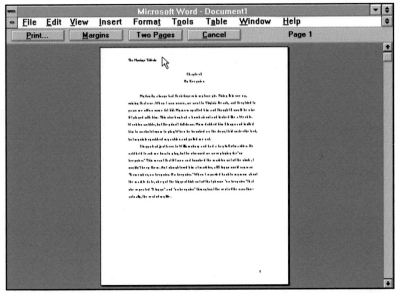

after

7. Click on **Close**.

This step confirms the header and closes the Header window. You don't see the header text in normal view. To see the header, you must preview the document or change to Page Layout view. See *TASK: Preview a document* or *TASK: Change to Page Layout view*. (The After screen shows a preview of the document.)

Use other options
You can include page numbers, dates, and graphics in the header. See *Using Word for Windows 2,* Special Edition, for information on all header options.

To create a header

1. Click on **View** in the menu bar.

2. Click on the **Header/Footer** command.

3. Click on the **Header** option.

4. Click on **OK**.

5. Type the text for the header.

6. Click on the **Close** button.

Don't see the header on page 1?
If you don't see a header on page 1, you might not have unchecked the Different First Page check box. Open the Header/Footer dialog box and turn off this option.

Edit a header

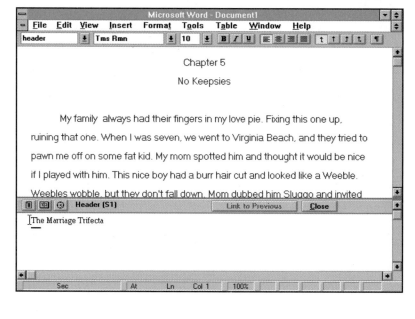

Oops!
Follow the same
procedure to change
the header back to its
original text.

1. **Click on** View.

   This step opens the View menu. You see a list of View commands.

2. **Click on Header/Footer.**

   This step selects the Header/Footer command and displays the Header/Footer dialog box. You use the same dialog box to create headers or footers.

3. **Click on Header.**

   This step selects the Header option.

4. **Click on OK.**

   In normal view, you see the Header window. The header you created appears in this window. The insertion point is at the beginning of the header text. (The Before screen shows this step.)

5. **Type Chapter 5:.**

   This is the additional text you want to print at the top of each page.

6. **Press the space bar.**

   This step inserts a space between the new text and the original text.

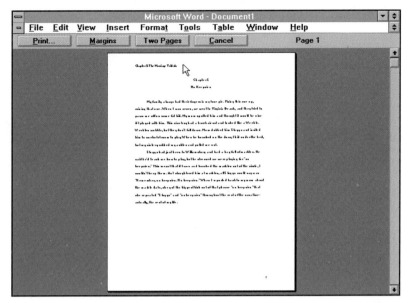

after

7. Click on **Close**.

   This step confirms the header and closes the Header window. You don't see the header text in normal view. To see the header, you must preview the document or change to Page Layout view. See *TASK: Preview a document* or *TASK: Change to Page Layout view.* (The After screen shows a preview of the document.)

Delete a header?
To delete a header, open the Header window, select all the text, press the Del key, and then close the Header window.

REVIEW

1. Click on **View** in the menu bar.

2. Click on the **Header/Footer** command.

3. Click on the **Header** option.

4. Click on **OK**.

5. Edit the header.

6. Click on the **Close** button.

To edit a header

Create a footer

before

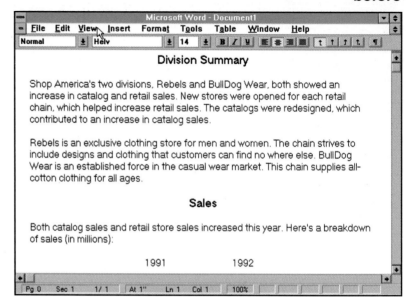

Oops!
To close the dialog box without creating a footer, click on Cancel in step 4.

1. **Click on View.**
   This step opens the View menu. You see a list of View commands.

2. **Click on Header/Footer.**
   This step selects the Header/Footer command and displays the Header/Footer dialog box. You use the same dialog box to create headers or footers.

3. **Click on Footer.**
   This step selects the Footer option.

4. **Click on Different First Page so that the check box does not have an X in it.**
   By default, Word for Windows does not display a footer on the first page of a document. This step turns off this option so that the footer appears on the first page.

5. **Click on OK.**
   In normal view, you see the Footer window. You type the text of the footer in this window.

6. **Type Annual Report.**
   This is the text you want to print at the bottom of each page.

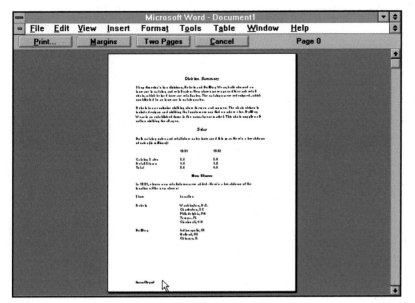

after

7. Click on **Close**.

This step confirms the footer and closes the Footer window. You don't see the footer text in normal view. To see the footer, you must preview the document or change to Page Layout view. See *TASK: Preview a document* or *TASK: Change to Page Layout view.* (The After screen shows a preview of the document.)

1. Click on **View** in the menu bar.

2. Click on the **Header/Footer** command.

3. Click on the **Footer** option.

4. Click on **OK**.

5. Type the text for the footer.

6. Click on the **Close** button.

Use other options
You can include page numbers, dates, and graphics in the footer. See *Using Word for Windows 2,* Special Edition, for information on all footer options.

To create a footer

Don't see the footer on page 1?
If you don't see a footer on page 1, you might not have unchecked the Different First Page check box. Open the Header/Footer dialog box and turn off this option.

Edit a footer

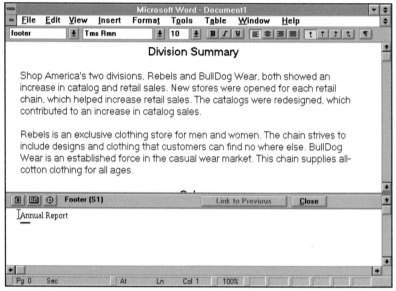

1. Click on **View**.

   This step opens the View menu. You see a list of View commands.

2. Click on **Header/Footer**.

   This step selects the Header/Footer command and displays the Header/Footer dialog box. You use the same dialog box to create headers or footers.

3. Click on **Footer**.

   This step selects the Footer option.

4. Click on **OK**.

   In normal view, you see the Footer window. The footer you created appears in this window. The insertion point is at the beginning of the footer text. (The Before screen shows this step.)

5. Press **End**.

   This step moves the insertion point to the end of the footer text.

6. Press **Tab** two times.

   This step moves the insertion point two tab stops. By default, Word for Windows provides a center tab and a right tab in headers and footers. This step moves the insertion point to the right tab stop.

7. Click the **Page Number** icon.

   This step inserts the page number at the right margin.

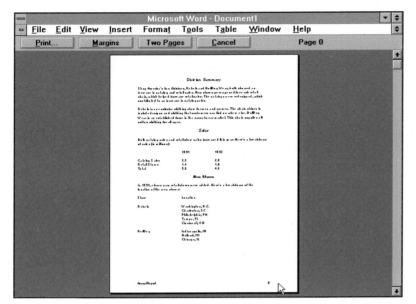

after

8. Click on **Close**.

   This step confirms the footer and closes the Footer window. You don't see the footer text in normal view. To see the footer, you must preview the document or change to Page Layout view. See *TASK: Preview a document* or *TASK: Change to Page Layout view*. (The After screen shows a preview of the document.)

REVIEW

1. Click on **View** in the menu bar.

2. Click on the **Header/Footer** command.

3. Click on the **Footer** option.

4. Click on **OK**.

5. Edit the footer.

6. Click on the **Close** button.

Delete a footer?
To delete a footer, open the Footer window, select all the text, press the Del key, and then close the Footer window.

To edit a footer

Number pages

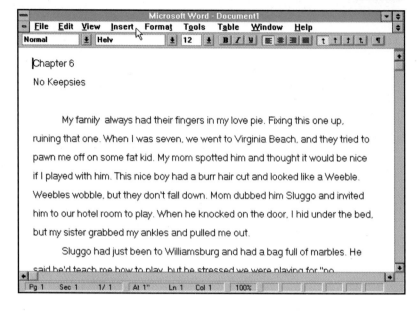

Oops!
If you change your mind, click on Cancel in step 5.

1. **Click on Insert.**

   This step opens the Insert menu. You see a list of Insert commands.

2. **Click on Page Numbers.**

   This step selects the Page Numbers command and displays the Page Numbers dialog box. When you add page numbers, you add them to a header or footer. (For more information on headers and footers, see *TASK: Add a header* or *TASK: Add a footer*.) You can specify whether to add the page numbers to the top of each page (to a header) or to the bottom of each page (to a footer). You also can specify the alignment (the default alignment is right).

3. **Click on OK.**

   This step accepts the default. Word for Windows creates a footer and adds the right-aligned page number to the footer. You cannot see the page numbers in normal view. To see the page numbers, you must preview the document or change to Page Layout view. See *TASK: Preview a document* or *TASK: Change to Page Layout view*. (The After screen shows a preview of the second page of the document.)

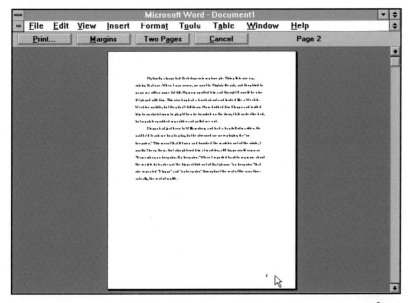

after

No page number on page 1?
By default, a page number does not appear on the first page. To display the page number on the first page, see *Using Word for Windows 2,* Special Edition.

To number pages

1. Click on **Insert** in the menu bar.

2. Click on the **Page Numbers** command.

3. Specify where you want the page number to appear: **Top of Page (Header)** or **Bottom or Page (Footer)**.

4. Select the alignment of the page number: **Left**, **Center**, or **Right**.

5. Click on **OK**.

Use other options
For complete information on all page numbering options, see *Using Word for Windows 2,* Special Edition.

Add a border to a paragraph

before

Oops!
To undo the formatting change, select the Edit Undo Formatting command immediately after making the change.

1. **Select the first paragraph.**

   This step tells Word for Windows what paragraph you want to surround with a border. For help selecting text, see *Task: Select text*.

2. **Click on Format.**

   This step opens the Format menu and displays a list of Format commands.

3. **Click on Border.**

   This step selects the Border command and displays the Border dialog box. In the Preset area, the Box option is selected.

4. **In the Line area, click on the first line style in the second column (a single, thin line).**

   This step tells Word for Windows what line style you want to use for the border. In the Sample area, you can see how the paragraph will look.

   You can select different line styles or create a drop shadow. For information on all dialog box options, see *Using Word for Windows 2*, Special Edition.

5. **Click on OK.**

   This step accepts the selected border and closes the dialog box. The paragraph remains selected.

6. **Click outside the selected paragraph.**

   This step deselects the paragraph.

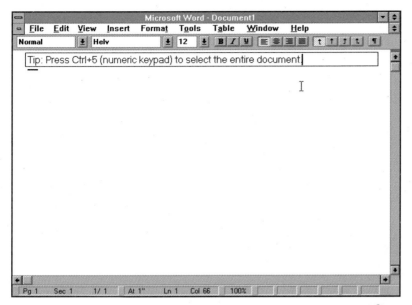

after

1. Select the paragraph(s) to which you want to add a border.

2. Click on **Format** in the menu bar.

3. Click on the **Border** command.

4. Click on the line style you want to use as the border.

5. Click on **OK**.

6. Click outside the selected paragraph(s).

To add a border to a paragraph

Add a line to a paragraph

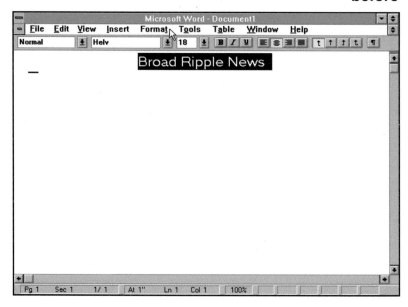

before

1. **Select the first paragraph.**

   This step tells Word for Windows what paragraph you want to format with a line. For help selecting text, see *Task: Select text*.

2. **Click on Format.**

   This step opens the Format menu and displays a list of Format commands.

3. **Click on Border.**

   This step selects the Border command and displays the Border dialog box.

4. **In the Border area, click on the bottom of the displayed paragraph.**

   This step tells Word for Windows where to place the line. Two arrows appear along the bottom of the paragraph. (No arrows should appear on any other sides of the paragraph.)

5. **In the Line area, click on the second line style in the second column (a single, thick line).**

   This step tells Word for Windows what line style to use for the border. In the Border area, you see a line along the selected border.

   You can select different line styles or create a drop shadow. For information on all dialog box options, see *Using Word for Windows 2,* Special Edition.

Easy **Word for Windo**

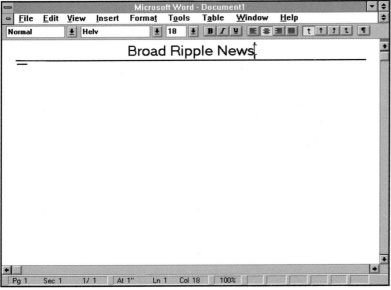

after

6. Click on **OK**.

   This step accepts the selected border and closes the dialog box.
   The paragraph remains selected.

7. Click outside the selected paragraph.

   This step deselects the text.

1. Select the paragraph(s) to which you want to add a line.

2. Click on **Format** in the menu bar.

3. Click on the **Border** command.

4. In the Border area, click on the side of the paragraph(s) where you want to add the line.

5. Click on the line style you want to use.

6. Click on **OK**.

7. Click outside the selected paragraph(s).

To add a line to a paragraph

Printing

This section covers the following tasks:

Select a printer

Display a document in Draft mode

Display a document in Page Layout view

Preview a document

Print a document

Select a printer

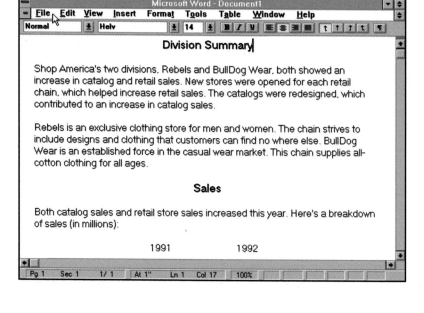

1. **Click on File in the menu bar.**

   This step opens the File menu. You see a list of File commands.

2. **Click on Print Setup.**

   This step selects the Print Setup command. You see a list of the printers you installed through Windows. (See your Windows manual for help with installing a printer.)

3. **Click on PostScript Printer on LPT1.OS2.**

   This step selects the PostScript printer. If you don't have this printer, select a printer you do have.

4. **Click on OK.**

   This step closes the dialog box. When you print the document, Word for Windows uses the printer you selected. Your printer selection also affects what fonts are available. See *Using Word for Windows 2,* Special Edition, for complete information on fonts.

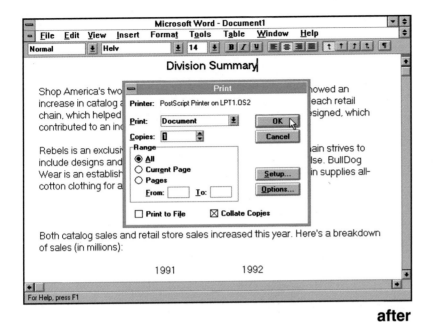

after

1. Click on **File** in the menu bar.

2. Click on the **Print Setup** command.

3. Click on the printer you want to use.

4. Click on **OK**.

To select a printer

Display a document in Draft mode

before

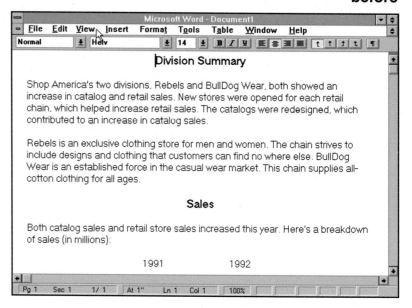

1. **Click on View in the menu bar.**

   This step opens the View menu. You see a list of View commands.

2. **Click on Draft.**

   This step selects the Draft command. You see the document in Draft mode. This mode does not display fonts or font attributes, but enables you to work more quickly.

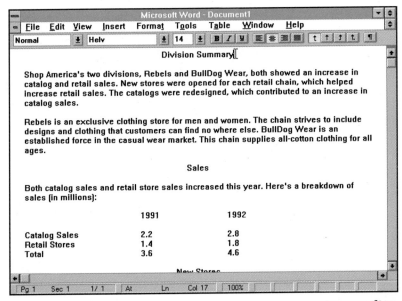

after

1. Click on **View** in the menu bar.

2. Click on the **Draft** command.

To display a document in Draft mode

Display a document in Page Layout view

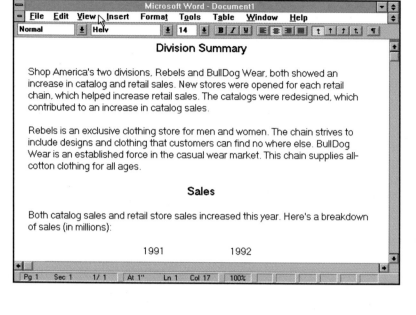

Microsoft Word - Document1

File Edit View Insert Format Tools Table Window Help

Normal | Helv | 14 | B I U | ☰ ☰ ☰ | ↑ ↑ ↑ ↑ | ¶

Division Summary

Shop America's two divisions, Rebels and BullDog Wear, both showed an increase in catalog and retail sales. New stores were opened for each retail chain, which helped increase retail sales. The catalogs were redesigned, which contributed to an increase in catalog sales.

Rebels is an exclusive clothing store for men and women. The chain strives to include designs and clothing that customers can find no where else. BullDog Wear is an established force in the casual wear market. This chain supplies all-cotton clothing for all ages.

Sales

Both catalog sales and retail store sales increased this year. Here's a breakdown of sales (in millions):

1991   1992

Pg 1   Sec 1   1/ 1   At 1"   Ln 1   Col 17   100%

Oops!
The Page Layout command is not a toggle. To turn off Page Layout view, you must select another view. To return to normal view, select the Normal command from the View menu.

1. **Click on View in the menu bar.**

   This step opens the View menu and displays a list of View commands.

2. **Click on Page Layout.**

   This step selects the Page Layout command. You see the document in Page Layout view. Items such as headers and footers appear in this view. Use Page Layout view when you are making many formatting changes and need to see the results.

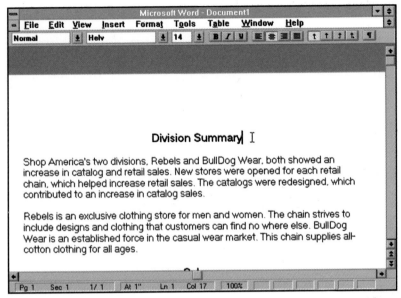

after

1. Click on **View** in the menu bar.

2. Click on the **Page Layout** command.

To display a document in Page Layout view

Preview a document

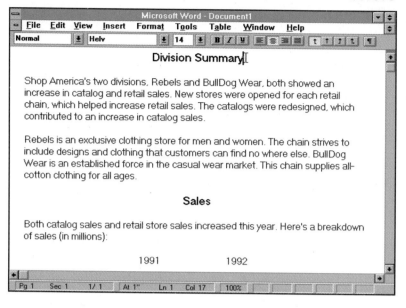

Oops!
To exit Print Preview, click on the Cancel button.

1. **Click on File in the menu bar.**

   This step opens the File menu and displays a list of File commands.

2. **Click on Print Preview.**

   This step selects the Print Preview command. You see a graphical representation of how your document will look when printed. You can change the margins or print from this view. See *Using Word for Windows 2,* Special Edition, for complete information.

3. **Click on Cancel.**

   This step returns you to the normal document view.

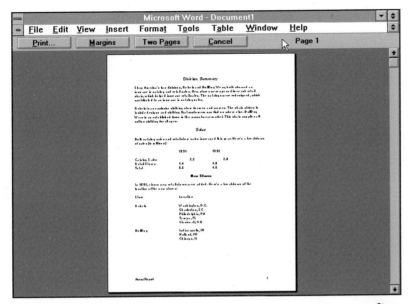

after

1. Click on **File** in the menu bar.

2. Click on the **Print Preview** command.

3. Click on the **Cancel** button.

To preview a document

Print a document

before

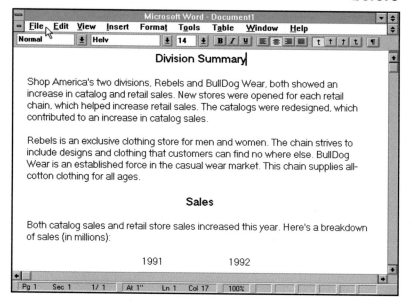

1. **Click on File in the menu bar.**

   This step opens the File menu and displays a list of File commands.

2. **Click on Print.**

   This step selects the Print command. You see the Print dialog box. This dialog box enables you to control what you print (the entire document, a range of pages, and so on), how many copies you print, and other options. See *Using Word for Windows 2,* Special Edition, for complete information on all options. (The After screen shows this step.)

3. **Click on OK.**

   The document prints.

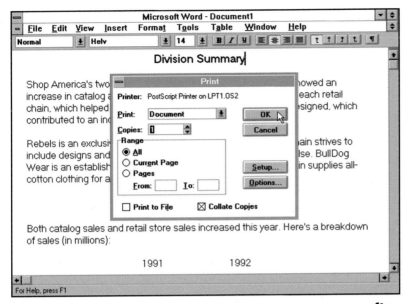

after

Cancel the print job
While the document is printing, you see a dialog box on-screen. Click on Cancel to cancel the print job.

1. Click on **File** in the menu bar.

2. Click on the **Print** command.

3. If necessary, change any print options.

4. Click on **OK**.

To print a document

Keyboard shortcut
Press the Ctrl+Shift+F12 key combination to select the Print command.

Reference

Quick Reference Guide

Keyboard Guide

Glossary

Easy **Word for Windows**

Quick Reference Guide

This section lists the menu commands and keyboard shortcuts for the most commonly used Word for Windows features:

Feature	Menu Command	Keyboard Shortcut
Bold	Format, Character	**Ctrl+B**
Center	Format, Paragraph	**Ctrl+E**
Close file	File, Close	**Ctrl+F4**
Cut text	Edit, Cut	**Ctrl+X**
Copy text	Edit, Copy	**Ctrl+C**
Date	Insert, Date and Time	
Exit	File, Exit	**Alt+F4**
Find	Edit, Find	
Font	Format, Character	**Ctrl+F, Ctrl+F**
Footer	View, Header/Footer	
Go to	Edit, Go To	**F5**
Hanging indent	Format, Paragraph	**Ctrl+T** (create) **Ctrl+G** (undo)
Header	View, Header/Footer	
Help	Help	**F1**
Indent	Format, Paragraph	**Ctrl+N** (create) **Ctrl+M** (undo)
Italic	Format, Character	**Ctrl+I**
Left align	Format, Paragraph	**Ctrl+L**
Line spacing	Format, Paragraph	
Margins	Format, Page Setup	
Move	Edit, Cut and then Edit, Paste	**Shift+Del, Shift+Ins**
New file	File, New	
Open file	File, Open	**Ctrl+F12**
Page break	Insert, Break, Page Break	**Ctrl+Enter**

Feature	Menu Command	Keyboard Shortcut
Page numbers	Insert, Page Numbers	
Paste text	Edit, Paste	Shift+Ins
Preview	File, Print Preview	
Print	File, Print	Ctrl+Shift+F12
Replace	Edit, Replace	
Ribbon	View, Ribbon	
Right align	Format, Paragraph	Ctrl+R
Ruler	View, Ruler	
Save	File, Save	Shift+F12
Save as	File, Save As	F12
Speller	Tools, Spelling	
Tabs	Format, Tabs	
Thesaurus	Tools, Thesaurus	Shift+F7
Underline	Format, Character	Ctrl+U
Undo	Edit, Undo	Alt+Backspace or Ctrl+Z

Keyboard Guide

Instead of using the mouse with Word for Windows, you can use the keyboard. This section covers some basic keyboard operations. The Quick Reference Guide also lists keyboard shortcuts. For complete instructions on using the keyboard, see *Using Word for Windows 2,* Special Edition.

To open a menu

Press the Alt key and then type the underlined letter in the menu name.

To select a menu command

1. Press the ↑ or ↓ key to move to the command you want to select.

2. Press Enter.

Or

Type the underlined letter in the menu command name.

To select a text box in a dialog box

Hold down the Alt key and type the underlined letter in the text box name.

To select a check box or option button in a dialog box

Hold down the Alt key and type the underlined letter in the check box or option button name.

To select an item in a list box

Hold down the Alt key and type the underlined letter in the list box name. Press the ↑ or ↓ key to select the item.

To select text

Hold down the Shift key and then press the arrow keys to highlight the text.

Glossary

Clipboard A temporary storage place for text or graphics. When you cut or copy text or graphics, the program stores that item in the Clipboard. The Clipboard is a Windows feature.

Control menu box The hyphen or box that appears at the left end of a window's title bar. Double-clicking on this box closes the window.

default Standard Word for Windows settings that are in effect each time you start the program.

dialog box A window that displays additional command options. Many times a dialog box reminds you of the consequence or result of a command and asks you to confirm that you want to go ahead with the action.

directory An index to the files stored on disk or a list of files. A directory is similar to a file cabinet; you can group files together in directories.

document window The area in which you type text. You can have more than one document window open at one time.

DOS An acronym for disk operating system. DOS manages the details of your system—storing and retrieving programs and files.

file The various individual reports, memos, databases, letters, and so on that you store on your hard disk (or floppy disks) for future use. The actual Word for Windows program is also stored in a file.

file name The name that you assign to a file when you store it to disk. A file name has two parts: the root and the extension. The root can include up to 8 characters. The extension can have up to 3 characters, usually indicates the file type, and is optional. The root and extension are separated by a period. For example, MEMO.DOC is a valid file name. MEMO is the root, and DOC is the extension.

floppy disk drive The door into your computer. The floppy disk drive enables you to put information onto the computer—onto the hard drive—and to take information off the computer—onto a floppy disk.

font The style, size, and typeface of a set of characters.

hard disk drive The device within your system unit that stores the programs and files with which you work. A hard disk drive is similar to a floppy disk drive except that a hard disk holds more information, stores and retrieves information much more quickly, and usually is not removable.

hard return A code the program inserts in the document when you press Enter. You use hard returns to end paragraphs or to insert blank lines.

icon A picture that represents a group window, an application, a document, or another element within a window.

insertion point A flashing vertical line that indicates where you will begin typing text, deleting text, selecting text, and so on.

menu An on-screen list of Word for Windows commands.

Microsoft Windows An operating environment that provides a graphical interface (rather than DOS). A graphical interface enables a user to learn a computer program more intuitively and to use a computer program more easily. You use Microsoft Windows to manage your computer system—to run programs, copy files, and so on.

mouse An input device that enables you to move the insertion point, select text, select menu commands, and perform other operations.

mouse pointer The on-screen graphic that moves when you move the mouse on a flat surface. The mouse pointer appears as an arrow in menus and dialog boxes and as an I-beam in the text area.

path name The route, through directories, to a program or document file. For example, the path name C:\WINWORD\DATA\REPORT.DOC includes these elements: the disk drive (C:), the root directory (\), the directory (WINWORD), the subdirectory (a directory within the first directory, DATA), and the file name (REPORT.DOC).

ribbon An on-screen option bar that enables you to make formatting changes (to change the font, font size, font style, and alignment). You can turn on or off the display of the ribbon.

root directory The main directory. All other directories are contained in the root directory.

ruler An on-screen option bar that enables you to make formatting changes (to change tabs, indents, and margins). You can turn on or off the display of the ruler.

scroll bars The bars at the bottom and right side of a document window. At the ends of each scroll bar are scroll arrows; click on any scroll arrow to scroll the window in that direction.

status bar The bottom line of the Word for Windows screen. This line displays messages, the location of the insertion point, the page number, and other information.

title bar The area of the document (or application) window that displays the name of the document (or application).

Toolbar An on-screen option bar that contains buttons you can use to access commonly used commands. You can turn on or off the display of the Toolbar.

window A rectangular area on-screen where you view an application or a document. A window can contain icons that represent applications, the application itself, or a document you created by using an application.

word wrap A feature that eliminates the need to press Enter each time you reach the right margin. Instead, Word for Windows "wraps" the word to the next line automatically.

Index

Index

Easy **WordPerfect for Window**

Index

Easy **WordPerfect for Window**